QUITO FEB 13 '76

SANTA CLARA COUNTY LIBRARY

. 3 3305 21058 5034

D1476646

746.41   MCKEE
            HAVASUPAI
            BASKETS & THEIR
            MAKERS...

612233

Santa Clara County Free Library

California

Alum Rock	Milpitas { Calaveras / Community Center / Sunnyhills
Campbell	
Cupertino	Morgan Hill
Gilroy	Saratoga { Quito / Village
Los Altos { Main / Woodland	Stanford-Escondido

Research Center-Cupertino

For Bookmobile Service, request schedule

HAVASUPAI BASKETS
AND THEIR MAKERS: 1930-1940

cKee, Barbara.
avasupai baskets and
heir makers, 1930-1940
1975]
3305210585034
J   07/10/12

Havasupai Baskets
and their Makers: 1930-1940

by Barbara and Edwin McKee

and Joyce Herold

Basket photographs by E. Tad Nichols

612233

NORTHLAND PRESS

SANTA CLARA COUNTY LIBRARY
SAN JOSE, CALIFORNIA

Copyright © 1975 by Edwin McKee, Barbara McKee and Joyce Herold

All Rights Reserved

FIRST PRINTING

ISBN 0-87358-134-2

Library of Congress Catalog Card Number 74-82364

Composed and Printed in the United States of America

Contents

Illustrations

Baskets

listed according to makers

Acknowledgments

IN THE PREPARATION of this book, the assistance and support of the Havasupai Tribal Council, and of many individuals in the tribe was greatly appreciated. Especially helpful was the use of the Havasupai Membership Roll of 1972, which was kindly arranged by Oscar Paya, chairman of the Tribal Council. Among the basketmakers who were interviewed and who contributed much information while the book was in preparation in 1973 were Edith Putesoy, Minnie Marshall, Ethel Jack, Viola Crook and Irene Walema.

Acknowledgement is gratefully made to Mr. Steve Hirst, tribal recorder, for furnishing a supplementary list of vital statistics on various members of the tribe, to Mr. Bill Willoughby, business manager of the Tribal Affairs Management Program, and to Mr. Charles Pitrat of the Bureau of Indian Affairs at Valentine for assistance. The encouragement of Dr. Edward B. Danson and Dr. William Lipe of the Museum of Northern Arizona at Flagstaff is appreciated, and thanks are extended to Charles T. Crockett, Acting Director, and Arminta Neal, Assistant Director, at the Denver Museum of Natural History for allowing Joyce Herold time and use of facilities for work on this project.

Others who have contributed to the development of this book and whose help is much appreciated are the following: E. Tad Nichols of Tucson, Arizona, who did an outstanding job of photographing all of the basketry, and his wife, Mary Jane, who assisted in this work; Mark Graede of the Museum of Northern Arizona who prepared the photographic prints; Curt Mast of Denver for preparing maps; Nancy Dillon and Arminta Neal who prepared the botanical drawings; Alfred Whiting of the Museum of Northern Arizona for providing access to his unpublished Havasupai research; and Laurance Herold who assisted in many ways.

Appreciative thanks are extended to Marsha Gallagher of the Anthropology Department of the Museum of Northern Arizona for helpful suggestions and criticisms of the manuscript.

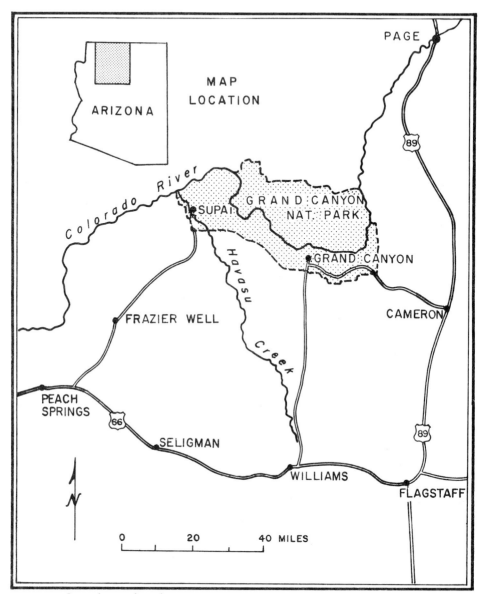

FIGURE I. Central part of northern Arizona showing Supai village in western Grand Canyon National Park.

Introduction

The Havasupai basket weavers described in this book are women of the Havasupai tribe who, during the first half of the 20th century, developed the art of basketmaking to a very high degree. Their baskets of that period are among the finest made by any of the North American Indians.

These people live on the floor of a narrow sheer-walled canyon that is a tributary of the Grand Canyon (figs. 1, 2). The walls are composed mostly of bright red, limy sandstone that forms a series of massive cliffs and ledges many hundreds of feet in height (fig. 3). A large stream of clear, blue-green water, beginning as a spring that rises from the valley floor about a mile above the Indian village, flows down the canyon. Below the village it forms a series of spectacular waterfalls, three of which are between 100 and 200 feet high (figs. 4, 7). Cottonwoods, willows and other water-loving trees everywhere form lush growth along the stream course.

The canyon and its stream are named Havasu and the Indian village in the canyon bottom is called Supai. *Pai* in their language means "people" so, literally translated, Havasupai are the people of Havasu or "people of the blue-green waters." At the main entrance to that part of the canyon where the village is located are two red sandstone pillars or monuments referred to as Wigleeva that are considered to be deities or spirits by the local Indians.

The Havasupai have for a long time lived primarily by farming and they have made good use of irrigation systems. They grow corn, beans, squash, sunflowers, melons and various fruits. In the early days their diet was supplemented with game obtained by hunting and with pinyon nuts and numerous seeds gathered on the plateau above. Likewise they made extensive use of native canyon plants such as the mescal or century plant. Wild foods have today largely been replaced by store-bought items.

Their homes, until the present decade when modern type houses have been introduced, were brush and log huts called *hawa'a* (fig. 5). They also spent much time in open-sided shelters during warm weather. A small brush and mud house (fig. 6) is still commonly used for taking sweat baths.

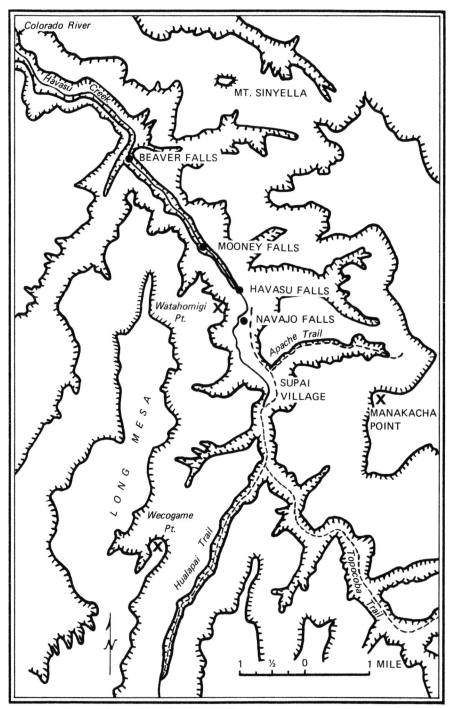

FIGURE 2. Havasu Canyon showing Supai village (center), waterfalls and principal trails.

Although a majority of the nearly 500 people in this tribe have homes in
Havasu Canyon, many of them live part of the time at Grand Canyon village
or among their relatives, the Hualapai, at Peach Springs to the west. Formerly
some of them resided farther east near the Little Colorado River and others lived
in the Grand Canyon near its eastern end. Most of them observed a seasonal
living cycle, spending summers in the canyon in order to farm and winters on
the forested plateau where there was an abundance of wood and native foods.

Frequently moving in and out of their canyon, the Havasupai have long
depended largely on their horses for trail transportation. Havasupai men excel
in horsemanship and most of the women are experienced riders. Mary Wescogame, known as Supai Mary (see figs. 28, 29), won many horse races at local
rodeos during the 1920s and 1930s. In those days two principal trails gave access
to Havasu Canyon; one, the Topocoba trail, about 12 miles long, began at the
east approach road from Grand Canyon village; the other, the Hualapai trail,
descended from the west. In the 1930s the U.S. mail was brought down by pack
horse twice weekly on the Topocoba trail. Today only the Hualapai trail is used
extensively and the mail comes that way. It is probably the only regular mail
route in the United States still using delivery by horse.

The introduction to the Havasupai people for Barbara and Edwin McKee
came in the late 1920s when they made visits to Supai village. From 1930 to

FIGURE 3. Cornfield on canyon floor at
Supai, 1929.

FIGURE 4. Mooney Falls, 186 feet, largest
waterfall in Havasu Canyon.

1940, Edwin McKee served as Park Naturalist at Grand Canyon National Park, and they lived on the south rim of the Grand Canyon where they became acquainted with many of the Havasupai who lived or visited there. It was then that the baskets illustrated in this book were collected.

There are 184 baskets in the collection. Most are still with the McKees. A few have been on display at the Musuem of Northern Arizona in Flagstaff for many years. Ultimately, the entire collection will be deposited at this museum, where Edwin McKee served for eleven years as Assistant Director. This seems to be an especially appropriate repository for the collection because of its location near the home of the Havasupai.

The collection includes utilitarian types of twined baskets, such as winnowing trays, pitch-covered water jars and burden baskets, as well as several cradleboards with wicker hoods. In the 1930s these articles were still in common use among the Havasupai. The bulk of the collection, however, consists of coiled trays, bowls and jars with geometric, plant or animal designs woven in black. Beautifully crafted baskets like these, which represented long hours of hard work, were usually made for sale.

FIGURE 5. Havasupai house or *hawa'a*, 1929, in Supai village (note log ladder).

The work of thirty-two Havasupai women is represented in the collection. Several weavers are responsible for a dozen or more baskets each, but others furnished only one or two. The majority are represented by a number somewhere between these two figures. Essentially all of the baskets were obtained directly from the makers by Barbara McKee, who also kept records of the makers' names and of the date of each acquisition. She also photographed most of the women.

In 1969, when the McKees asked Joyce Herold, an anthropologist at the Denver Museum of Natural History who specializes in basketry, to catalogue and appraise the collection, its importance and that of its existing documentation soon became obvious. They then conceived the idea of a book combining Herold's technical and comparative approach with their own considerable experience in the Grand Canyon region, and the knowledge of living basketmakers. The McKees knew that this knowledge could be obtained because, in the 1960s and early 1970s they had discovered on a series of trips to Havasu Canyon that a number of basketmakers were still active, eager to see and discuss photographs of their baskets, and willing to share their understanding with others.

FIGURE 6. Sweat house near Havasu Creek, May 1974.

FIGURE 7. Havasu Falls in 1929.

The History of Havasupai Basketmaking

Early basketmaking—the old tradition: The art of basketmaking among the Havasupai apparently dates back very far, and in aboriginal times their baskets took the place of metal ware or pottery as the most important household containers. Basketry was used traditionally in the forms of burden carriers, water bottles, bowls, trays and the hoods of cradleboards. Few written records are available concerning early basketmaking activities, largely because historic records of all types, concerning these people, are scarce. This is doubtless the result of their extremely isolated location. The early Spanish padres and the military, geological and railroad exploring parties so prominent in Grand Canyon history scarcely noted the existence of these Indians, much less their crafts.

The first detailed account of Havasupai life came from Dr. Frank Hamilton Cushing, an ethnologist who visited the Havasupai in 1881 accompanied by a Zuni Indian guide. Cushing briefly recorded numerous evidences of the weaving and use of baskets. The Havasupai women, he observed, "are wonderfully apt and graceful in the use of the hand in making baskets and preparing food" (1882, p. 50). Baskets were used in parching sunflower seeds and in serving food (1882, p. 54, 56). "Large panniers, slung over the forehead or shoulders with a broad strap of raw-hide, are used in collecting food . . . ; and certain huge, small-necked, round-bottomed basket bottles serve as canteens and water jars" (1882, p. 56). Their art is "mostly confined to the patterns on their basket-work and the painting on their bows and arrows. The basket-work, by virtue of the regular arrangement of the splints, is often beautiful" (1882, p. 70).

Although the antiquity of the twined basketry, as described by Cushing, is certain, the early history of the coiling technique of basketmaking among the Havasupai is somewhat vague. A coiled jar-shaped boiling basket used in the old days has been variously described. According to Spier (1928, p. 124–25), a boiling basket with a globular, open-mouthed, bowl form was formerly made by either twining or coiling. A jar-shaped boiling basket made by coiling is shown in an 1887 work by Cushing (1887, fig. 503); and a similar boiling basket in use by the Havasupai as late at 1899 was observed by James (1903, p. 163). Several

I

other forms of early coiling, collected by Voth in Hopi country between 1893 and 1898, reside in the Field Museum of Natural History collections (Whiting, 1942, p. 4–6). A small cylindrical bowl and at least three small trays were ascribed by the Hopi to the "Cahoninos," i.e., the Havasupai or Hualapai. They "represent very early examples of Havasupai coil work" and "cannot be differentiated in technique or materials from the later coil baskets" (Whiting, 1942, p. 6). These baskets were old and worn when collected and show that Havasupai knowledge of coiling extends back many years previous to 1890.

The coiling technique seems to have been little used, however, until about 1880 or slightly later when production of a new style of coiled tray became popular among the Hopi (Whiting, 1942, p. 6). The development between about 1870 and 1890 of a particularly attractive, large, relatively shallow, black-decorated, coiled tray was stimulated by a number of factors: importation of more effective tools (metal awls) and better materials used for decoration (longer devil's claw), knowledge of a new style of basketry introduced by the Yavapais, encouragement from school teachers and increased commercial demand from both Hopi and white people. With the appearance of this popular tray type, the development of Havasupai decorative coiled basketry begins and can be traced continuously to the present. It apparently culminated in the work of the 1930s, illustrated in this book.

Turn-of-the-century basketmaking—innovations: In the years following Cushing's visit, the life of the Havasupai changed rapidly. A reservation was established, a school and teacher were brought in, and visits by tourists began. One well-known visitor, George Wharton James, was an avid basket fancier whose Havasupai collection and photographs were featured in turn-of-the-century compendiums of Indian baskets (Mason, 1904; James, 1903). A good photographic record and a small collection of baskets, now at the Denver Museum of Natural History, was left by J. M. Bratley, who taught school at Supai in 1900 and 1901. From these and other museum sources the major characteristics of Havasupai basketry, circa 1890 to 1910, can be determined.

Basket production flourished in the early 1900s. Although some forms, like the boiling basket, had long been replaced by metal containers, most twined articles were retained unchanged and still functioned importantly in the household. All of the burden baskets examined had simple black geometric bands, interrupted at the back where the carrier's body would obscure the pattern. Some twined trays had similar simple design bands in black. Water jars had typical biconical or squat, globular shapes with small mouths. A few specimens lacked pinyon pitch waterproofing. A new form had an hourglass shape with the upper part large and open mouthed, forming an elevated bowl. This form resembles a non-Indian "compote" dish, from which it may have been modeled.

Many of the new type of large, finely woven, coiled trays were being made for trade with the Hopi and Navajo Indians and for sale to white men. According to James (1903, p. 63), "a good specimen is eagerly sought after and highly prized." Among the Hopi, coiled baskets were finding a ready market amounting to a veritable fad. Many early photographs of Hopi dances and house interiors show the black-decorated baskets, easily distinguished from the more thickly coiled, brightly colored Hopi baskets.

Most coiled baskets from this period were circular trays. Those examined ranged from twelve to sixteen inches in diameter and curved gradually from a flat base to a height of one to four inches. In general they were larger and deeper than the average tray of the 1930s. Aberrant tray shapes with constricted bases or everted rims were produced occasionally, and one flat plaque is known. The bowl form was apparently little developed. A deep form "more or less cylindrical, or the rim turning in or tending toward a spherical form" is described by Mason (1904, p. 517). An additional coiled form, little known and probably only from this period, was a squat, flat-bottomed globular jar, bottle necked and closed with a small flat lid attached at one side.

All coiling was done in a counter-clockwise direction using a three rod, triangular foundation, i.e., three sticks aligned with two below and one above. Though very regular in coil and stitch, this early coiling was not particularly fine in texture; its four to six coils and nine to thirteen stitches per inch compare poorly with most of the work of the 1930s.

In contrast to the spare, banded designs of Havasupai twined ware, coiled baskets displayed designs which relied to a great extent on borrowed elements. Havasupai coiled basketry designs of all periods closely resemble those of the Yavapai and Western Apache, and, as noted earlier, the influence of the Yavapai, at least, extends back prior to 1890. Because the construction techniques, as well as the designs, used by the three peoples are so similar, many baskets are difficult to identify positively without some information about their origin.

"The designs are often striking," wrote James (1903, p. 63). The major geometric motifs and arrangements of later years, such as multi-pointed centers and encircling bands of double fretlines, triangles and zigzags, were much in evidence. Diamonds and spiralling and radiating lines of various types appeared, and occasionally animal forms were used, including human beings, deer, and horses. Generally designs were more limited in number and more massive than in later baskets, although some finely delineated complex patterns appeared.

A false braid or herringbone rim was emphasized by James as a diagnostic trait separating Havasupai baskets from very similar Yavapai and Western Apache baskets (1903, p. 116, 166–67). Only about a third of the 1890–1910 baskets examined, however, had this type of rim. Most rims were in plain color. Still, many more herringbone rims appeared during this period than later.

A diagnostic trait of this period is the greater use of color; aniline-dyed purple, green and especially red appeared in a minor way alongside black in about one-fourth of the baskets. Various colors were used, but mostly different shades of red, as mentioned by Mason (1904, p. 517). It was claimed by James (1903, p. 230) that aniline dyes would not be used by Indians if they did not think white purchasers preferred them, and he refused to buy any baskets with color from the Havasupai.

Thus, the decades before and after 1900 saw continuation of the traditions in twining and the beginning and expansion of a new development in basketry among the Havasupai, that of the coiling of highly decorative trays for sale. Quantity of coiling may have outweighed quality. Along with experimentation in form and color, a foundation of techniques, forms and designs of coiled basketry was firmly laid.

Early twentieth century basketmaking—a plateau: Information about basketry during the period 1910 to 1930 comes primarily from the classic work *Havasupai Ethnography* by Leslie Spier. The field work for this study was conducted during 1918, 1919 and 1921.

Even though European ways had made significant inroads into Havasupai culture, Spier noted a continued domestic role for baskets:

> A dozen or so may be found in each household; two or three burden baskets, half a dozen trays holding foodstuffs, one or two parching trays, a water bottle or two. . . . Basketry is entirely women's work, to which they devote most of their spare time, particularly the long midday period when household duties are light. Wherever women gather, basketry may be seen; the hostess working at her products, the guests plucking and preparing twigs from the nearby bushes, or more commonly helping the hostess at such tasks. Women do not usually carry their unfinished wares further than a neighbor's camp; not even the coiled baskets which are worked on only intermittently and regarded much as our women do embroidery. Twined baskets were worked on more consecutively. . . . Expertness is recognized and prized; a few women are widely acknowledged as preeminent (Spier, 1928, p. 124).

Factory-made utensils still had not reached Havasu Canyon in quantity, nor were they well suited for wild plant gathering or food preparation, the methods of which had changed but little.

Twining continued to be the most common technique and examples of twined burden baskets, water bottles, trays and parching trays were noted by Spier, who made the following observations on form and decorations. Three sizes of burden baskets, ranging from twenty-four to fourteen inches in diameter, were made to suit the needs of women, half-grown girls and small girls, respectively. Most burden baskets were decorated with one to three simple black design bands of ticks, mostly oblique, with or without a baseline of zigzag lines or of triangles. The majority of water bottles were biconical with pointed bases and narrow mouths. These measured about 13½ inches in diameter at the waist and 10 inches high. Water bottles were also made with flattened or rounded bases and some were hourglass shaped. The twined trays, used to hold foodstuffs, consisted of relatively large trays, about 15 inches wide and 3½ inches deep, and small trays, twelve inches wide and two inches deep. Trays had black decorations of narrow-line bands, ticked or zigzagged, or a central circular area filled solid. After much usage the large trays, with a protective facing added, became parching trays (Spier, 1928, pp. 127–28, 137).

Coiled baskets of this period all took a circular tray form, about the same size as twined trays, but somewhat flatter (Spier, 1928, p. 127). Thus, coiled trays were generally shallower than in the preceding period; some specimens from the late 1920s are nearly flat. The texture of the baskets became slightly finer, and by the late 1920s some makers were producing specimens with up to fourteen stitches and seven coils per inch. Most rims were plain self-rims, but a few baskets were finished with alternating plain and black stitches, a three-strand stitch, or a herringbone stitch (Spier, 1928, pp. 135–36).

An examination of the few documented museum specimens available indicates that the decoration of coiled baskets had changed very little from that of the immediately preceding periods. The design motifs and arrangements on these baskets are nearly identical to those used earlier. As before, the majority of the coiled baskets were produced for sale or trade. Spier viewed the decoration on these trade baskets as being somewhat cluttered in appearance and he contrasted this with the more simply and sparsely designed baskets preferred by the Havasupai for their own use (1928, p. 138).

The trade of coiled baskets to the Hopi Indians probably had slackened considerably by the early 1920s and is scarcely mentioned by Spier (1928, p. 244). As large numbers of visitors reached the Grand Canyon both by train and by automobile, however, sales to tourists became increasingly important. Indian handiwork had long been sold in hotels and stores of the area, but now these crafts were featured at such places as the Hopi House and other shops of the Fred Harvey Company. Demonstrations and sale items centered on the Hopi and Navajo Indians (Hughes, 1967, pp. 112–13). Apparently, the less pictur-esque Havasupai attracted interest only through their coiled basketry, and this was scarce and expensive compared to the wares of many other Indians.

In summary, basketmaking in the early decades of the twentieth century continued trends of the preceding periods, remaining on a kind of plateau at the level achieved by the turn-of-the-century makers. The major twined and coiled forms, together with their decorations, were retained with little change. A decline of some aberrant shapes, the use of dyed color and herringbone rims may illustrate changing preferences of the basketmakers and of their clientele, now almost entirely non-Indian.

Basketmaking in the thirties—the peak: Havasupai coiled baskets made from 1929 to 1940 represent a high point in Southwestern basketry. As the years around 1900 had seen an "explosion" in quantity production of an innovative basketry type, so the 1930s saw a dramatic upturn in quality and variety of the craft.

Basketry was made in considerable quantities in the 1930s (Douglas, 1931, p. 3). Twined utility baskets retained their old characteristics but played a role of diminishing importance. Basketmakers turned their attention more and more to the coiling of baskets made primarily for the purpose of sale. They began doing much better work technically than before. Materials were prepared with great care in smaller sizes so that, in general, the texture of weaving became finer. Some weavers achieved fine and superfine textures. Others turned to forms demanding much time and skill.

A broadened range of forms, shapes and sizes was produced during the 1930s. Plaques and bowls joined trays in common production and jars, double bowls and several variations of basic shapes appeared. Trays generally were more shallow and smaller than previously, but great extremes of size were reached in all forms.

The inventory of designs was greatly expanded through both individual in-vention and copying from diverse sources. To the basic designs which continued from about 1890 were added many motifs derived from plants, animals and cul-tural objects. Although geometric designs never lost great favor, natural history designs gained more attention than ever before. More complex and intricate pat-terns were used, many of them exhibiting outstanding balance and symmetry.

The above changes indicate a greater awareness by basketmakers that their work was no longer restricted to use in Supai kitchens or display at Hopi dance plazas, but that they also were decorating fine Anglo homes. The popular plaque form was designed for use as a wall decoration.

The changes in basketry were not due solely to the increased economic incentive, but also to broadened personal and cultural views resulting from an ever growing contact with the outside world through education, employment and other means. However, the basketmakers on the whole were conservative and the changes which did occur were more often than not new adaptations of old ways.

Midcentury basketmaking—the art in decline: The art of coiled basketmaking had diminished little in the early to mid-forties when Bert Robinson, an authority on Southwest Indian basketry and author of *The Basket Weavers of Arizona,* observed basketmaking in Havasu Canyon. He stated, "The Havasupai women rank high among the weavers of fine baskets in Arizona" (Robinson, 1954, p. 132). His book illustrates forms similar to those of the thirties, including circular and oval trays, said to be quite common, and circular bowls, described as mostly small. Designs are shown to be closely similar to those of the previous decade, including stepped spirals, encircling zigzags and fret-lines and stylized ducks. Robinson (1954, p. 134) observed: "The outstanding characteristics of these baskets are the beauty of design and smoothness and evenness of contour, all of which are the result of careful preparation of weaving material, as well as of craftsmanship." These baskets apparently were made primarily for sale to the tourist trade, and commonly were shipped to the purchaser by mail.

A significant change from basketmaking of the thirties, observed by Robinson, was an extreme scarcity by midcentury of twined utility baskets of all types. The picture of a weaver with newly twined deep, open-mouthed bowls and a shallow tray was shown by Robinson (1954, p. 133, Pl. K), however. Coiling also may have begun to be less common at the time of his observations. Despite praise of Havasupai workmanship, the oval tray which he illustrates as an example of the contemporary basketry seems to be of inferior quality in the technical sense, being coiled somewhat irregularly and sewn with widely spaced stitches (Robinson, 1954, Pl. LXI).

By 1950 Havasupai basketmaking had declined drastically, not only in the production of utility ware, but also in the making of coiled ware. Documentation of this decline is furnished by C. L. Smithson, an ethnographer working among the Havasupai from 1950 to 1952. She states:

Interest in [basketweaving] has so fallen off that, in 1950, only half a dozen women were actively occupied in making baskets despite the fact that their supply never equals tourist demand. It was said that the work of a few other women who had tried basket weaving at one time or another was too inferior in quality for sale. Most of the older women are able to make twined baskets for their own use, but seldom do. Apparently no one has twined a burden basket for some years, and only three examples of this type were observed about the village. The only other basket type seen in use was a broad, shallow tray convenient for winnowing seeds, parching corn, pinyon nuts or seeds, and for drying peaches, figs, or other fruit (Smithson, 1959, p. 143).

Cradleboards, which had wickerwork hoods, did continue in general use (Smithson, 1959, pp. 146–47).

Coiled baskets were still being produced for sale in a variety of sizes. One weaver is known to have made baskets ranging from miniatures only "two to three inches in diameter up to trays one foot or more across" (Smithson, 1959, p. 147). As for ornamentation, even though few basketmakers were active at this time, Smithson (1959, p. 145) observed that three of them were especially skilled in decorating their baskets. The designs used included the familiar geometric and life forms common in earlier baskets. More interesting are the examples cited by Smithson of one woman who produced a new design by copying a four-leaf clover and of another, a beginning weaver, who consulted a book on Papago basketry to copy designs (1959, p. 145). The willingness to try a new design, whether original or copied, seems to have been typical of Havasupai non-utilitarian coiled basketry from the beginnings through today. Because of this, the design development has been anything but static.

The decline in basketmaking continued, with production probably reaching a low ebb during the period 1960 to 1967 (Bateman, 1972, p. 48). Only a few small baskets were being produced (Tanner, 1968, p. 24). Thus, Havasupai basketmaking went in thirty years from a peak of excellence to near extinction. Tragically commonplace in the history of Indian crafts and arts, such declines seem to accompany the accelerated mixing of native Indian culture with the Anglo-American culture. In the case of the Havasupai, the period of 1940 to about 1967 brought expanded outside economic opportunities, together with strong social pressures disrupting the traditional culture. Among the innovations which reached the Canyon after World War II were electricity, a tractor, improved mail services and a more affluent, modern life style. However, by the 1960s employment in the Canyon still was very limited and many people had moved to nearby towns.

The difficult work of basketmaking earned few rewards for Havasupai women in the midcentury period as prices paid for baskets remained low and social recognition of craftsmen was minor. A comparable situation is described by Bateman (1972, p. 53–56) at Peach Spring among the Hualapai. Their basketmaking activities were brought to an even lower ebb, earlier than those of their canyon relatives. That Havasupai women had produced such good baskets for so long a time into the twentieth century was largely a result of their isolation; but, at last, in the 1960s, the art of fine basketmaking was nearly lost.

Basketmaking in the seventies—the art revived: Each year in the present decade several thousand people hike or ride horses into Havasu Canyon. Growing numbers of these visitors buy baskets at the tribally-operated restaurant or directly from the makers. Simplified, smaller versions of the old twined utility baskets are available in some quantity. The toy burden baskets, water jars (without the traditional covering of pinyon pitch), small trays and round bowls are represented, but they lack the evenly-sized sewing elements, tight twining, double-coil rims and other refinements of the past. Even so, these crude vessels indicate a revival of basketmaking. The weavers are responding, quickly and in the easiest way possible, to an increased market for tourist curios at relatively high prices.

A number of practiced weavers, many of whom have been inactive for a score or more years, have resumed coiling baskets. Furthermore, several young women have recently taken up the craft, and others have expressed a desire to learn. A class in basketmaking has been discussed. The revival of interest in fine coiling has doubtless been spurred by a sharp rise in the prices offered for such baskets. An appreciation of "things Indian" has swept the country, and baskets have come into vogue more than at any time since the turn of the century. Supai baskets are much in demand because of their superior quality and rarity. Moreover, tribal consciousness and pride in cultural heritage, including arts and crafts, is on the upsurge among the Havasupai. Approval and appreciation from kinsmen and friends seem to be incentives to good basketmaking.

Seventeen active basketmakers live in Supai village at present, and several others live in nearby towns. Present basketmakers in Havasu Canyon include Viola Crook, Katie Hamadreek, Grace Hanna, Ida Iditicava, Ethel Jack, Maude Jones, Florence Marshall, Gertrude Marshall, Minnie Marshall, Caroline Putesoy, Edith Putesoy, Bessie Rogers, Cora Rogers, Mae Tilousi, Elizabeth Uqualla, Mecca Uqualla and Flossie Wescogame. Five of these are young women who have turned to basketmaking, mostly coiling, in the past four years. Seven were producing baskets as long ago as the 1930s. Fourteen of the makers do coiled work, seven exclusively. Twining is done by eleven and at least six make cradleboards.

After a winter of making baskets, the major weavers are likely to have on hand a total of about twenty-five or thirty baskets, the majority being twined ware of small size. Local people, including Indians, buy many of the baskets; dealers and tourists purchase most of those remaining. Demand is heavy and many pieces are ordered ahead of time. Cradleboards, in both small and large sizes, are produced for local use as well as for sale.

Most of the shapes popular forty years ago appear in modern coiled work, but smaller sizes generally are preferred. Workmanship ranges from the loose, heavy, irregular texture of the novice or the elderly weaver with poor eyesight to a relatively fine weave (sixteen stitches and six coils per inch) produced by the experienced makers. Typically work today is comparable only to the coarser work of the 1930s; no modern baskets attain the fine and superfine textures found in the best products of that period. Many old designs, both geometric and realistic, are on the baskets, but some of the younger weavers use new motifs copied from other crafts and other tribes. Patterns tend to be more crowded and complex than formerly, though some extremely simple patterns reflect the limited experience of the new weavers or the tastes of the old ones.

The Process of Basketmaking

Materials used: Supai baskets are made entirely of materials obtained from plants,* both native and cultivated, that grow in Havasu Canyon. The availability of these materials is of prime importance in the production of baskets. Various materials can serve the same purpose in Supai weaving, and individual basketmakers have different preferences.

The small tree known as catclaw, *Acacia gregii* (fig. 8), is a preferred twining material because its wood is very strong. This desert tree is common in Havasu Canyon and attains a height of 20 feet. Catclaw twigs are split and scraped for use as weaving elements in twined baskets and cradleboard hoods.

The shrub squawberry, *Rhus trilobata* (fig. 9), was not only an alternate

*Plant names, both common and scientific, as used in this section, were kindly checked by W. B. McDougall, Curator of Botany at the Museum of Northern Arizona, Flagstaff. They follow usage in his book *Grand Canyon Wild Flowers,* published in 1964.

FIGURE 8. Catclaw: *Acacia greggii. aromatica (Rhus trilobata)* FIGURE 9. Squawberry: *Rhus*

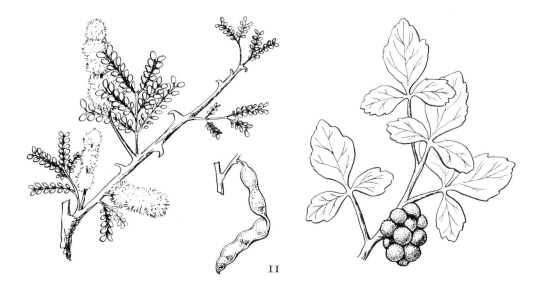

preferred source for woven elements in twining, but also was commonly used in coiled basketry. Long, straight shoots of this shrub, when split, form smooth sewing splints that stay a lustrous white, in contrast to other materials which may become discolored with age. The squawberry has aromatic foliage and bright red berries, and it is common on canyon slopes.

The Fremont cottonwood, *Populus fremontii* (fig. 10), provided material for both coiling and twining, but was considered inferior material for the latter. This tree is conspicuous along streams and frequently grows to fifty feet and sometimes one hundred feet in height. Its twigs provide light, tough weaving material which turns slightly brown with age.

Numerous species of willow, *Salix,* grow adjacent to streams and along ephemeral water courses in the vicinity of Supai. They are recognized as distinct plants and are given individual names in the Havasupai language. Two species, *Salix goodingii* (fig. 11) and *Salix bonplandiana,* provide material for basket-makers (Whiting, 1942). Willow was apparently once considered inferior for twining but has been much used for this work in recent decades. The shoots are important in coiled basketry. They are used whole as foundation rods and split as sewing splints. The desert willow, *Chilopsis linearis,* which resembles the true willow, but is a botanically different plant, also provides foundation material for coiled work.

Apache plume, *Fallugia paradoxa* (fig. 12), is a handsome, much-branched

FIGURE 10. Fremont cottonwood: *Populus fremontii.*

FIGURE 11. Goodding willow: *Salix gooddingii.*

shrub that forms dense growth on hillsides and in valleys. The slender branches are sometimes utilized for rims of twined baskets and for crosspieces on cradle-boards. Arrowweed, *Pluchea sericea,* a shrub which grows profusely in stream beds and in saline soils, is similarly used.

Other native shrubs that have been used in basketry are service berry, *Amelanchier utahensis,* and cliff rose, *Cowania mexicana.* Twigs of serviceberry form heavy rims on twined ware, and the bark of cliff rose is used for pads on cradleboards.

The black designs on Havasupai baskets are woven with the split mature pods of a plant usually known in Arizona as devil's claw, *Proboscidea parviflora* (fig. 13). This annual herb has a bushy growth with large-lobed leaves and showy flowers. The fruit ends in a long incurved, hooked beak, with a tough black or dark grey covering. This covering is stripped to form sewing elements for basket designs.

A variety of devil's claw with hooks about six to eight inches long is native to Havasu Canyon, and an introduced variety with hooks about four inches longer is commonly cultivated. The latter yields adequate crops of the black claws for local use, so few basketmakers gather the smaller wild form. The introduced form is planted in rows about a yard apart and requires little care.

Gathering and preparing materials: All basket materials, except devil's claw, are gathered in the form of young branches or shoots, cut in lengths of two to

FIGURE 12. Apache-plume: *Fallugia paradoxa.*

FIGURE 13. Devil's claw: *Proboscidea parviflora (martynia parviflora)*

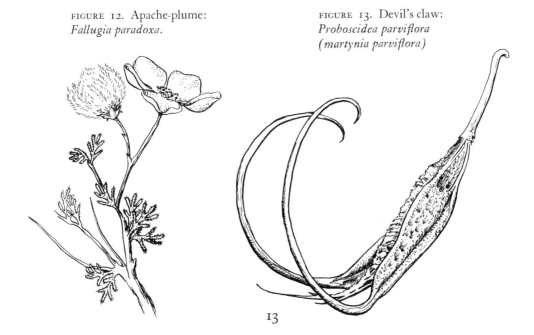

13

three feet (fig. 14). Each plant has an optimum time for gathering, normally when its shoots are most pliable and straight. Willow is best gathered in late August, but can also be taken in March or April. Cottonwood is gathered mostly in early spring, but sometimes is collected in July and August when it is considered to be "ripe." Both squawberry and catclaw plants are checked regularly for they must be kept pruned or they will not send out new, usable shoots. Mature devil's claws are harvested in September.

Shoots that have been collected are partially stripped of leaves, bundled conveniently and stored for use. The basketmakers must plan ahead to have a supply of materials at hand for times of the year when fresh shoots cannot be gathered.

FIGURE 14. Minnie Marshall gathering willow shoots.

Sticks to be used inside coils as foundation rods are rubbed and scraped with a knife to remove the bark and to make them smooth and even. The sewing elements for coiling, referred to as splints, are prepared by splitting the shoots into three parts as follows: a three way cut about two inches long is made in the small end of a shoot which has been stripped of leaves and bark. One part of the shoot is held between the front teeth, and each of the other two parts is pulled out by hand (fig. 15). The weaver's fingers guide the two splints gradually until they separate down the entire length from the splint held by the teeth. If equal tension is maintained, three even portions result.

Each splint is thinned by removing the inner pith. In a process similar to that described above, the weaver's teeth hold the pith, while one hand pulls

FIGURE 15. The splitting of a willow shoot into three sewing elements.

15

away the pliable outer layer and the other hand guides and supports the splint. Again, even tension in separating the parts results in long, evenly-thinned splints. Splints at this stage of preparation usually are bundled, wrapped and stored for future use.

Devil's claw is split in the following way: when the pod is dry, the hook of the claw is pushed back and broken with the palm of the hand, then twisted with the hand and torn off. Segments of the covering next are lifted with a knife at the end of the claw and pulled back, stripping the claw and forming splints which are the length of the claw.

Plain splints for coiling undergo further careful preparation when a basket is under way. They are scraped with a knife and are meticulously sized. Some weavers draw each strip through a hole punched in a tin can to bring it to a desired size, using a gradation of five to six holes to produce uniform strips of proper sizes for baskets ranging from miniature to large. Twining materials are prepared in much the same way as those used in the coiling, except that the bark is left on all elements and the splints are not so finely cleaned and sized.

Few people know or appreciate the specialized knowledge, manipulative skill and long, tedious hours which go into choosing, gathering and preparing basketry materials. The fineness of rods and splints is a major determinant of weaving texture. Therefore, to be an expert weaver one must first be an expert preparator, for any inept or sloppy methods will result in an inferior basket.

Dyes are rare on Havasupai baskets today. Designs are normally executed in the natural black of the devil's claw, which is cultivated and always in plentiful supply.

Dyes were used more frequently in the past, particularly in the period around 1900. They continued to appear after that time, but became much less common. For example, only two of the 183 baskets in the McKee collection have dyed elements, indicating that the use of dyes during the 1930s was unusual. Two elderly weavers of that period who are known to have used dyes are Swechakecha Watahomigie, maker of no. 104 in the McKee collection, and Taschikva Big Jim. Both of these women may have been remembering and copying the techniques of an earlier time.

Color has also appeared sporadically on the baskets of Hualapai women who have married into the Havasupai group but who have retained the old Hualapai practice of decorating primarily with bright aniline dyes. Ella Kaska and Dottie Watahomigie are in this group.

The dyes used on Havasupai baskets probably included native ones as well as aniline. The two baskets in the McKee collection with dyed elements give evidence for both types. Basket no. 104 has a gold that was most likely obtained from hollygrape (*Berberis sp.*). The roots of this plant, well known to today's basketmakers, produce a brilliant yellow dye. The red on basket no. 104 and the black of basket no. 149 were probably produced by commercial aniline dyes.

Learning basketmaking: Basket weaving always has been women's work, but men sometimes gather the materials. One man in the 1930s, moreover, was skilled enough to help his handicapped wife, Mabel Barney, in beginning her coiled baskets, for he would often weave as far as the start of the design.

Girls who were so inclined commonly learned basketmaking by watching a member of their family or a neighbor weave. Neither techniques nor designs were taught as such, but assistance in the actual process was given when needed. Serious development of weaving skills generally began only after a woman took up married life in her own home. A few weavers did not take up the craft until they were relatively old, even middle aged.

The technique of twining: Havasupai basketmakers differentiate two basketry techniques: rough weave and fine weave. The first refers to twining, which is used primarily for utility ware; and the second to coiling, which produces the decorative or "fancy" ware made primarily for ornaments or for sale.

Baskets made by twining are represented in the McKee collection by three trays, six water jars, and one burden basket. The making of twined baskets has been described fully by Spier (1928, pp. 129–34) and by Bateman (1972, pp. 31–36). Briefly, the process begins with several pliable sticks laid at right angles across each other and bound together with a double split weaving element. More sticks are inserted to form a spoke-like foundation. These are joined together in clockwise direction by the two twining elements, one of which crosses over and the other crosses under the sticks, alternating with top to bottom at regular intervals. In plain twining the elements cross over a single stick each time; in diagonal twining, which is the type most often used, the elements cross over two and under two sticks. Three-strand twining, with an interval of three or four sticks, is used to strengthen bases, curves or rims, or to change the weave decoratively. The rim consists of a double round of sticks split in half, laid inside and outside of the twined edge and bound on with an overcast stitch.

Trays intended for parching use are given a heat resistant coating of cooked peach or apricot pulp. This mixture is rubbed liberally into the interstices of the inner basket surface and allowed to dry. A similar coating usually begins the waterproofing of water jars. In these, red clay is then rubbed on the outer surface, and finally a coating of pinyon pitch is applied. The pitch is boiled in a container and poured inside the jar which is then rotated so that the pitch reaches all crevices. Pitch is swabbed on the outside with a cloth tied to a stick. Sometimes hot stones are rolled around inside the jar to further force the melted pitch into the basketry. Such a coating is tough and impervious to water.

The technique of coiling: In Havasupai coiling, a flexible element is sewn around and through a foundation of three sticks arranged in triangular formation (fig. 16). From the beginning point, the foundation and sewing progresses continuously in a counter-clockwise, or right-to-left, direction. Consecutive coils or rounds are joined to each other by the sewing element, which is brought up over the coil and inserted into a hole pierced through the top part of the previous coil.

The primary tool used in coiling is a short, strong, fine-pointed awl. Most modern weavers make their own awl by grinding down an ice pick, or by inserting a nail, fork tine or similar metal piece into a wooden handle. A weaver also has frequent recourse to a knife, used for trimming materials to get an exact fit and to make sharp points on sewing elements.

Previous to weaving, the splints normally are made flexible by soaking in water. Water frequently is applied with the fingers along the length of the foundation sticks during weaving.

A weaver usually sits and supports the bottom of the coiling on her upper leg near the knee. Facing the weaver is the working side of the basket; the awl and sewing elements are inserted from this side. The working side always forms the top of shallow trays and plaques and the outside of bowls and jars. The opposite side is called the rough side.

FIGURE 16. Diagram of
Havasupai coiling technique.

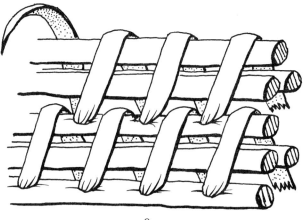

The start of coiling is exacting work. The small end of a foundation stick is first made pliable by chewing it with the front teeth for a distance of about $2\frac{1}{2}$ inches and then working it back and forth in the fingers. Two other sticks are similarly prepared for a distance of about $1\frac{1}{2}$ inches. At the point where pliability begins, the longer piece is wrapped and tied around the shorter ones and pulled tight. A hole is put through the center of this knot with an awl, and a fine sewing splint inserted from the front is pulled through except for the final half inch. The splint is brought around from the back and inserted into the awl hole again, over the starting end of the splint, catching it and holding it tightly. Still a third stitch is brought around through the hole to secure the end and it is then cut off. Now, with the lengths of the three foundation sticks arranged, two below and one above and protruding to the left, the weaver is ready to continue sewing in that direction.

After the first round, the weaver pushes the awl between the stitches and through the top stick of the coil below. The leading end of the sewing element, kept pointed with a diagonal cut, is brought without twisting from the back and inserted through the hole with the right-hand fingers. The end is grasped from the back and pulled through so that a tight encircling stitch is completed.

When a sewing element terminates, its end may be left protruding from the awl hole at the back of the coil. Later, when dry, these ends are removed by cutting with a knife, rubbing with the hands, or rubbing with a corn cob. Alternatively, the terminal end may be bent toward the left on the back of the foundation rods and caught under the new splint.

The end of a new splint is inserted at the back and caught either between the back two rods and the front one or underneath all three rods. If design stitches are desired, the new splint is made from devil's claw.

As each foundation rod terminates, a new one is trimmed to fit, inserted into the group of sticks, and held fast by the pressure of stitches around it. A curve or turn upward in the basket wall is accomplished by aligning the new coil slightly forward of the previous coil and angling the awl holes upward; whereas, an outward curve requires a more outward coil position and downward awl punch. As the pressure used in holding the sticks must be firm and constant and the punch of the awl strong and true, the weaver's hands and fingers are often strained and battered. Basketmaking is not only skilled work, but also hard work.

The execution of design: Havasupai weavers of the 1930s conceived and completely planned basket designs in their minds before starting work. Pattern drawings generally were not used.

The transfer of a design from the weaver's mind to a basket takes place slowly, stitch after stitch and round after round, as the basket grows from the center out. If the pattern is to be even and symmetrical, each design stitch must be placed correctly. Each round calls for a different relationship of black and plain, because the concentric coils gradually increase in circumference as the work progresses.

The weaver's eye is her major guide, sometimes aided by measures of distance, such as stitch counts and sized sticks laid over the work. A small piece of devil's claw inserted between stitches may mark the place where a design should start or end in the next round. Many mistakes are corrected by cutting the stitches with a knife, pulling them out and redoing the section.

Rim treatment in coiling: When the design and shape of a basket have been completed to the maker's satisfaction, the basket is ready for termination. The last coil forming the rim of the basket may be carried out in any of several ways.

Most baskets (93 percent of the coiled baskets in the collection) have a "self-rim," that is, the regular coiling stitch continues. In the final 1 to 1½ inches of the rim, the top foundation stick and the lower two sticks are tapered down so

FIGURE 17. Coiled basketry shapes: (a) trays

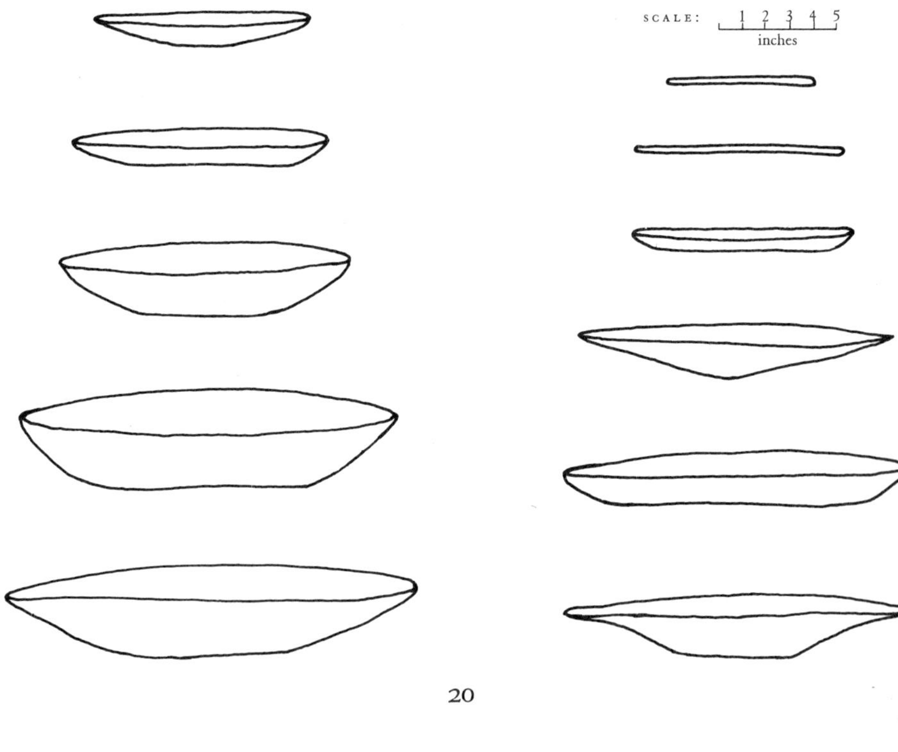

SCALE: 1 2 3 4 5
inches

that the coil becomes gradually smaller and smoothly diminishes to its end. In some baskets several additional back stitches anchor the end.

Most self-rims are plain or carry the last row of design stitches. In 12 percent of all coiled baskets in the collection, however, the self-rim is set off by being completely black. Two baskets are finished with alternating black and plain segments of self-rim.

A two-strand overcast rim technique, in which black and plain sewing elements alternate in a regular coiling stitch, appears in 4 percent of the collection's coiled baskets. The effect achieved by this technique is that of a ticked self-rim. Examples include jar no. 4, bowl no. 75, and tray no. 146.

In one basket (no. 49), a single-strand, overcast stitch was added in two directions over the final coil giving a cross-stitch effect. On two baskets (no. 53, no. 91) by Lina Iditicava, a false braid, or herringbone, rim was used. In this technique, a single sewing element was passed alternately forward, for a regular coiling stitch, and then backward four spaces, for a stitch under only the top foundation rod. This figure eight sewing process produced an obliquely woven, or braided, effect.

(b) bowls

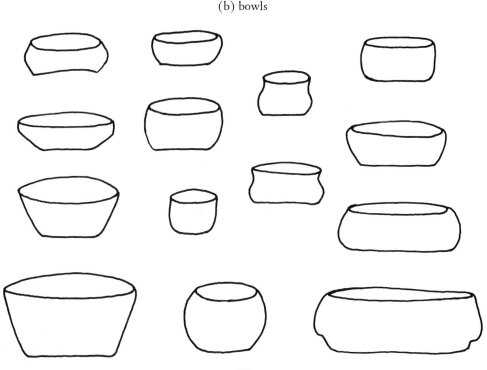

Shape and size of coiled baskets: The range in coiled ware shapes represented in the McKee collection is illustrated in figs. 17a-d. Trays, bowls, jars and a few miscellaneous forms are included. Sizes range from miniatures of a few inches to super-sized trays nearly two feet wide.

Trays are the most common basket form, numbering ninety-five, or 55 percent of the coiled baskets. Eighty percent of the trays are circular, ranging from 5¾ inches to 22 inches in maximum diameter, with an average size of about 11¾ inches.

Oval shape characterizes 20 percent of the trays. They are more uniform in size than the circular trays and most of them measure ten to fifteen inches in length. A few reach 20½ inches. Width normally is about 2/3, or slightly more, of the length.

Flat or essentially flat trays, called plaques, make up slightly more than 1/3 of the trays in the collection. The remainder have measurable depths ranging from 1 inch to 3¼ inches, but usually no more than 2 inches. These baskets, which are termed shallow trays, exhibit a wide variety of shapes. Bases may be flat or curved, merging either abruptly or gradually with straight or curved

(c) double bowls

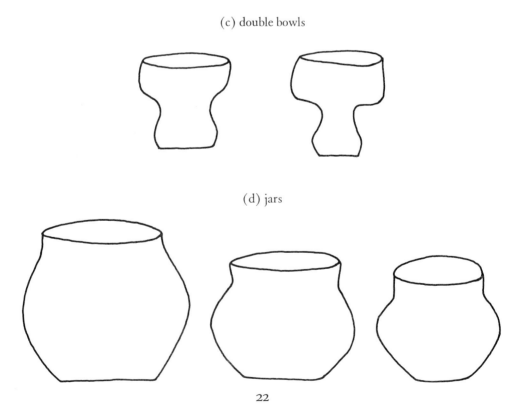

(d) jars

walls. Rims can curve either slightly inward or outward. Plaques and shallow trays are illustrated in fig. 17a, which clearly shows the wide variety in wall conformation of the latter tray type.

Bowls were only slightly less popular than trays in the 1930s. The collection includes seventy bowls or 40 percent of the coiled baskets. Most bowls are circular (71 percent); the remainder are oval. The range in bowl sizes illustrates the variety of functions which these baskets can serve: show piece miniatures, $2\frac{1}{2}$ to 4 inches in diameter, contrast with large storage baskets up to fifteen inches in width. Oval bowls are generally larger than circular ones, ranging from 15 inches to $5\frac{1}{2}$ inches in width, with a median of $7\frac{1}{2}$ inches.

As fig. 17b shows, both open-mouthed and globular bowls are formed of a variety of components. They may have flat or rounded bases, straight or curved walls, and incurved or everted rims. Bowls tend to be low, from $1\frac{1}{2}$ inches to $3\frac{1}{2}$ inches, with only a few of the largest bowls attaining heights of four to five inches or the maximum of nine inches.

The double bowl (fig. 17c) is one of the few eccentric forms developed in Havasupai basketry. A small, lower bowl is connected through a constricted neck with an upper, larger, open mouthed bowl. The effect is that of a bowl on a pedestal; however, the upper bowl does not have a separate base, and the form is hollow so it functions in its entirety as a vase-like container. Most double bowls are circular with the "pedestal" comprising two-thirds of the total height. One specimen is oval and on a very low "pedestal" (no. 58).

A twined version of the double bowl apparently was popular in the late 1800s and appears with some frequency in museum collections of that period. However, by the 1930s, few Supai women made this form. The four examples in this collection (no. 12, no. 13, no. 14, no. 15) range from $4\frac{1}{2}$ inches to $6\frac{3}{4}$ inches in mouth diameter and $5\frac{1}{4}$ inches to $6\frac{1}{2}$ inches in height.

In addition to the double bowls referred to, there is one "true" pedestal bowl in the collection (no. 11). In this specimen a flattened base extends into a short, curving support for a squat, open-mouthed bowl, complete with its own base. Another unusual bowl form is the distinct conical shape of the miniature no. 50.

A seldom-made jar form completes the inventory of Havasupai basketry shapes. Each of the six jars in the collection is a variation of a deep, circular form with flat base, curving walls, rounded shoulder, and short neck (fig. 17d). Most are wide mouthed with slightly outcurving rims. Ranging from $6\frac{1}{2}$ inches to 11 inches in shoulder diameter and from six inches to fifteen inches in height, the jars are medium sized in comparison with those commonly produced by the Yavapai and Western Apache.

The texture of coiled baskets: Havasupai baskets range from coarse to very fine in the texture of their coiled surfaces. Such differences are a function of the size of foundation sticks, width of sewing elements and closeness of stitches. Relative texture is commonly measured by counting the number of coils and stitches per inch in representative sections of basket wall.

Baskets of the 1930s show a range of from 3½ to 10 coils and 8 to 24 stitches per inch. A large majority (69 percent) have six or seven coils per inch. Larger coils (3½ to 5 per inch) occur in 12 percent of the baskets, and smaller coils (eight to ten per inch) in 19 percent. The ultimate in fine coiling is seen in no. 38, no. 44, no. 54, and no. 55, all of which are small bowls.

Stitch counts of fifteen to nineteen per inch characterize most baskets (64 percent). The remainder of the baskets are about equally divided between coarser (eight to fourteen stitches per inch) and finer (twenty to twenty-four stitches per inch) stitching. The latter group can be classed as "fine" in texture, and its upper limits, including twelve baskets with twenty-two to twenty-four stitches per inch, as "superfine" in texture.

The fine and superfine textures occur in both trays and bowls. All examples are small or miniature-sized baskets. On the other hand, the coarsest textures normally occur in the largest baskets, especially the bowl forms.

Time involved in basketmaking: Questions relative to the length of time required to make a particular plaque or bowl generally lead to no very meaningful or tangible reply—mainly because even though the time of beginning and completion of the weaving might be known, the actual working time in between these dates might differ greatly according to circumstances and the habits of the individual weaver. A general conclusion reached by Barbara McKee in the 1930s was that most of the decorated baskets were treated by the Havasupai women much as crocheting and other fancy handwork is done by the Anglo-American woman, that is, basketwork was carried on when leisure time was available and the spirit moved.

Modern weavers often look forward to a few hours of basketwork after completion of their morning household chores. Basketwork may be done along with friends, inside or out-of-doors, in the daytime or nighttime. One weaver spoke of becoming so absorbed in putting in design and so curious to see "how it would come out" that she devoted every free moment to completion of a basket. Other weavers work in a more desultory way. One woman took a year to make a large coiled tray; another regularly produces a small bowl or tray in two weeks.

Basket Designs

THE MAKERS OF BASKETS are primarily concerned with the process and craftsmanship, but other people focus on the finished product, particularly its appearance. The form, shape, texture, and rim treatment all affect one's aesthetic sense, but it is the decorative designs woven into the baskets that illustrate best the maker's artistry and record her culture and natural surroundings.

Several of the basketmakers represented in this collection have discussed with the authors their understanding of the designs. Their ideas and descriptions, as they apply to the basket collection, are treated in sections of the book that are devoted to individual basketmakers. In no case did informants imply any symbolism; these designs do not have magico-religious meaning, nor do they tell stories. Even though some are based on vivid imagery, designs are merely decorations in the baskets.

The weavers reproduced time and again, in a variety of ways, the motifs and patterns seen on their mothers' and grandmothers' work. Thus, they maintained traditional Havasupai design, the history of which was discussed earlier. Basketmakers sometimes work together and frequently see and discuss each other's baskets, sharing their knowledge about methods of preparing and making baskets. No formal Havasupai design exists, and weavers view each individual as the sole authority on her own creation.

Life forms: Animals, plants, and other natural phenomena are abundantly represented among the designs in Havasupai baskets of the 1930s. Such interest is to be expected considering the familiarity of these people with objects of natural history. However, the extent to which these designs are used is remarkable when the difficulties of making them are considered. Similar figures are common on Yavapai basketry, both early and recent, and so may have had an influence on the Havasupai weavers.

The principal types of animal life represented in Supai basketry are mammals, birds, insects, and reptiles. Naturalistic forms occur on thirty-four baskets and highly stylized ones on six. Large native mammals include mountain sheep, distinguished by big curving horns, and deer identified by short tails and divided hooves. Horses, being intimately related to the Supai way of life, are sometimes included in the designs of baskets, but dogs have been given scant recognition. Another mammal recorded in baskets of this collection is the bat, illustrated on a plaque by Mabel Barney.

Chief among mammals, of course, is the human being. Two baskets by Mamie Watahomigie Chick show standing figures in front silhouette, with arms raised and at sides. Males have spread legs and females short skirts. Three fingers are shown on each hand, except in one example where fingers are lacking (no. 147). Edith Putesoy made a unique design consisting of the head of a Supai man, outlined in side view and complete with bearded chin and feathers in hair.

Among the birds, eagles and falcons seem to be especially popular, because birds of this type, with tapering, pointed wings and triangular tails, have been recognized on thirteen baskets. Second in abundance among the birds are ducks, which are readily recognized by their distinctive side view shape. Wild ducks are seen occasionally along Havasu Creek by the women, but the curved, elongated neck on some of the "duck" motifs is reminiscent of the swan. This bird is exotic to the Supai, so influence from magazine illustrations or from needlework patterns is to be suspected.

The horned owl, fairly common in the region, is included in at least two baskets by Dottie Watahomigie, who does a good job of illustrating the characteristic front-view form despite its complexity. Finally, a bird on basket no. 114 made by Stella Yunosi has been identified by Edith Putesoy, her daughter, as a roadrunner. The roadrunner, though not common in this area, occurs locally and has a very distinctive shape with long tail, short wings and powerful legs used in running.

The only insect noted among designs of Havasupai baskets in the collection is the butterfly, but it obviously is popular, and occurs on eight baskets, representing the work of six different weavers. Butterflies are made with the four wings extended; some butterflies show antennae. It is perhaps expecting too much to attempt recognition of particular species of butterflies among the designs; however, judging from shape, several butterflies by Dottie Watahomigie probably were inspired by the abundance of large gaudy swallowtails near Supai village. Four highly abstract representations of a butterfly (no. 101) also occur in the collection.

Although snakes of several species are not uncommon in Havasu Canyon and environs, their portrayal in basket design by these Indians is not recorded. In contrast, lizards of various shapes and sizes are fairly common. Which particular lizard a weaver may have visualized when making one of these designs is not certain, but one example was identified definitely as a chuckwalla by Minnie Marshall (no. 158). Because the chuckwalla is the largest species in the area and has approximately the shape illustrated, it may well have been the model.

Dottie Watahomigie, of all the weavers who contributed to this basket collection, seems to have been the most enthusiastic user of animal motifs. She employed lizard designs so often that her friends Viola Crook and Ethel Jack say they "used to tease her about always making lizards." But she also made excellent butterflies, owls, as stated above, and included what probably was a dog. Mabel Barney also deserves recognition for her good portrayal of wildlife, including horses and bats. Elsie Sinyella on many of her baskets made birds of various types.

Elements of design derived from the plant kingdom are fairly common in Havasupai basketry. Many banded and radiating patterns composed of curving triangular shapes are said to represent leaves and are identified as such by Edith and her mother, Stella Yunosi. Although most of the "leaves" are impressionistic, a basket design by Mecca Uqualla includes large, well-formed leaves resembling those of the maple. Various kinds of trees are suggested by the motif on at least seven baskets and flowers occur on three. More unusual but also more distinctive plants are represented by a cactus (no. 140, maker unknown), a cattail (no. 37, Edith Putesoy), and a corn plant (no. 160, Mabel Barney).

"Like a tree, Christmas tree," is the name assigned by Edith Putesoy to a radial motif made up of stacked hollow crosses(or it may be visualized as a type of ladder). This highly abstract motif, which is used more often on bowls (nine examples) than on trays (two examples), may expand in width as it radiates up or out. Good examples occur on no. 13, no. 52, and no. 140. A different, stylized version of a tree is probably depicted in the outlined, branched figure on jar no. 2.

Other natural phenomena: Natural phenomena of the inorganic world, including wind, lightning, stars and rocks, are well represented as motifs for Havasupai basket designs.

The "star" is defined by various basketmakers as a zigzag-edged motif having five points. It is the most common of center ornaments for trays and plaques, and occurs on fourteen baskets. Stars are woven in black or negatively in white. Designs similar to the "star," but with four points form the centers in nine baskets. Six and seven-pointed "stars" are also represented. There are numerous other related multi-pointed motifs, but these fall into the leaf or flower group of designs.

"Lightning" as used on seven baskets was pointed out by several informants. It consists of a zigzag, stepped line, either in the form of a broad radial zigzag (no. 14, no. 57) or a double narrow-line zigzag (spirals on no. 93, banded on no. 75). Many similar broad or double zigzags occur on bowls and trays (fifteen in all), but whether all of these depict lightning is not clear.

In contrast to the variety of zigzags used for lightning, "wind" is fairly well defined as a single-line, stepped spiral, used repetitively, mostly on trays and plaques, in either clockwise or counterclockwise direction. The Havasupai expression for this design is *sequitaba;* it refers to "wind," rather than "whirlwind," as tourists commonly call this motif. Such spiralling single-line designs occur on eleven trays and five bowls, good examples of which are no. 22, no. 44, no. 93, no. 119, no. 128, and no. 156. Stella Yunosi and her daughter, Edith, especially favored this motif.

Geological features have been identified only in the baskets of Ethel Jack. She stated that "broken rocks at the canyon" are shown by a series of stepped triangles on her basket no. 45, and "hills" are portrayed by two long indented lines in no. 159.

Cultural features: A common form is a line of triangles arranged radially with points toward the base or center of a basket. This apparently ancient motif is generally referred to as "arrowheads." It appears on twelve baskets; no. 2, no. 10, no. 86 and no. 143 are good examples. A variation with the arrowheads divided laterally in the center occurs four times (e.g. no. 36 by Dottie Watahomigie).

The "trail" motif which depicts the familiar man-made pathways traversing canyonlands of the Havasupai country, consists of a fret-line or squared meander, used radially. It is included on nine bowls and trays; it may be simple (no. 92), more complex (no. 9), in paired, opposed lines (no. 122), or in negative design (no. 98).

Several little-used geometric motifs have been given names by some informants and apparently are patterned after cultural objects. "Railroad tracks" is a straight radial in no. 106 by Mabel Barney and forms the incomplete outer motif in no. 150 by Ethel Jack. "Ladder" appears radially in bowls no. 12, by Dottie Watahomigie, and no. 27, Stella Yunosi. "Chain" appears as a band in no. 66 (maker unknown). Closely related to Supai life is *cathok,* the important, early-type burden basket, shown in a complex trianguloid motif by Stella Yunosi in no. 145. "Boxes" were also made by Stella (no. 3, no. 146).

The swastika motif, in which arms rotate clockwise, is represented in three bowls. It was readily identified as a swastika by modern informants and according to Loren Sinyella is considered a "peace symbol." Because the swastika is one of the earliest known symbols in many parts of the world, its time and place of origin, and its possible significance to early Supai basketmakers is obscure.

Unnamed geometric motifs: The bulk of designs on Havasupai baskets have geometric forms that have not been given names by the basketmakers. Such unnamed motifs form the entire decoration on about a third of the coiled baskets in this collection and occur together with named motifs on many others.

There are three classic band designs which are used with more frequency than any other motif by the Havasupai. One, a simple, encircling, stepped-zigzag pattern occurs on fifty-three baskets and on all forms. Zigzags may be narrow or broad single lines (no. 125, no. 154), but most commonly are formed of double narrow lines (no. 67, no. 108). Some are formed of elongated blocks (no. 97); others are outlined (no. 83, outer), negative (no. 85, no. 110), or aligned point-to-point to form diamond networks (no. 21, no. 103).

A second type of band, consisting of stepped triangles-in-line, is extremely popular, and appears on thirty-eight coiled baskets and one burden basket. The triangles may be separated (no. 37, no. 157 center), or opposed (no. 96) along a line, although they mostly adjoin one another and are aligned in the same direction. Two bands closely opposed may form a negative zigzag between them (no. 152).

In the third type of band design, an encircling fretline (a meander with right angle steps) is used. This variety occurs on sixteen trays, two bowls, and a burden basket. In most baskets the frets are double lined (no. 69, no. 96 outer). They may be located anywhere from a central to a terminal position on a basket wall, and in a few baskets function as framing lines (e.g. no. 147 by Mamie Watahomigie). A single-line fret was referred to by one basketmaker as a "corral."

Several much-used panel or radial-type geometric motifs are not named. On eight bowls and trays checkerboards (alternate ticks of black on plain, row-on-row) take the form of zigzags (no. 25), radials (no. 157), or broad panels (no. 62). The checkerboard motif is framed and repeated in an overall checkerboard pattern on basket no. 4 by Stella Yunosi, and it covers the entire surface on another of her baskets (no. 118).

A distinctive radial motif, used on four baskets, might be described as a broad side-barbed line (no. 39). The barbs face to the right. This motif may be related to "arrowheads."

No name is known for the most traditional design of all—parallel narrow lines joined with slanted lines, i.e., an obliquely-hachured band. On twined ware the slant is upward to the right (no. 163), but on coiled ware it is to the left (no. 51, no. 112). Three bowls and three trays show this motif in banded arrangement. A "boxed" variant is in no. 99 by Stella Yunosi. Equally as important on twined baskets is the related single-line band with oblique pendant lines. Such slanting lines result naturally from the twining technique, as water jar no. 165 shows. By changing the color of twining strands, a weaver easily produces oblique ticks or lines.

A black circular center occurs in fourteen trays. It is of modest proportions in most baskets and serves as an origin point for spirals, zigzags, or straight radials (no. 130, no. 148, no. 177).

Isolated diamond shapes are used on eight baskets, the most elaborate of which is no. 9. Lines of diamonds occur on eight baskets, reaching a peak development in the centered diamond radials of jar no. 5.

Havasupai designs include comparatively few of the small individual motifs so common as space fillers on baskets of the Yavapai and Western Apache basketmakers. Names are not known for the small equilateral cross (no. 25, no. 114) and its hollow variant (no. 105, no. 144), nor for the blocked-"X" motif (no. 73), or the chevron "V" motif (no. 23).

Basketmakers

represented in this collection
arranged alphabetically

SCALE OF PHOTOGRAPHS

All the baskets illustrated in the following pictures are at one-fourth actual size except where labeled otherwise. Exceptions consist primarily of burden baskets, water bottles, cradleboards, and utility ware.

The text accompanying the weavers and their baskets is divided into two parts: (1) personal recollections by Barbara and Edwin McKee and historical data, (2) technical commentary on the baskets by Joyce Herold.

Wherever the name of a basket design appears in quotes, it is a descriptive term applied by the weavers.

The basketmakers discussed in this book are arranged in general to show family ties, with mothers followed by their daughters and sisters next to each other. The following relationships are noted:

Mother	Daughters
Stella Yunosi	Edith Putesoy, Josie Watahomigie
Mary Wescogame	Viola Crook, Ethel Jack
Clara Wescogame	Minnie Marshall
Suteluija Spoonhead	Elsie Sinyella, Clara Wescogame
Molly Mulgulo	Mecca Uqualla

THE BASKETS
THE BASKETMAKERS

IDA UQUALLA

1910–

Ida Uqualla, daughter of Joe Jones and Eunice Spoonhead (*To hót ta*), is one of the most expert basketmakers among the Havasupai. She went to school at Ft. Mohave. After her marriage to Edgar Uqualla, she lived at the Grand Canyon where he was working during the 1930s. Recently she has made her home in Williams, Arizona and also in Supai.

Ida made a few excellent coiled baskets, often using a flower design. Her other designs are mostly geometric. In the 1930s she did not restrict herself to making baskets of one shape, but, in addition to the round plaques, also made oval and bowl-shaped varieties.

FIGURE 18. Ida Uqualla weaving plaque.

FIGURE 19. Ida Uqualla and children.

THE FEW AVAILABLE SPECIMENS of this basketmaker illustrate uniformly skillful manupulation of both materials and design. Her small plaque (no. 142) is among the most finely textured of Havasupai baskets. Traditional geometric motifs encircle or radiate from the basket centers, sometimes in bold simplicity (no. 142), and at other times with delicate intricacy (no. 157). Two trays made in 1934 (no. 86 and no. 92) have strikingly similar texture, with large coils (4½ to 5 per inch), but fine stitching (eighteen per inch). Similar design elements occur in each, but a remarkable difference in overall effect results from the change in position of the negative design band. The motifs around the edge of no. 88 have been referred to by other weavers as "not Indian . . . something like a flower . . . could be copied from a book or a beadwork design."

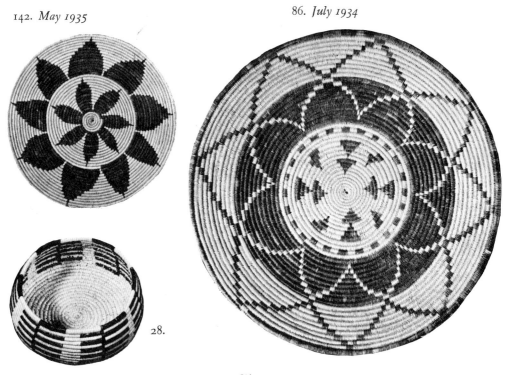

142. *May 1935*

86. *July 1934*

28.

92. *1934*

157. *September 1935*

88.

LINA MANÁKAJA CHIKAPANEGA IDITICAVA
1893–1968

Lina Iditicava spent most of her life in Supai where she went to school as a young child. Her first husband was Jess Chikapanega who often took what baskets she made to the tourist stores at Grand Canyon village to sell. Later Lina was married to Duke Iditicava. She was known as one of the best basket-makers among the Havasupai and other basketweavers acknowledged her very fine workmanship. She continued making excellent baskets until her death. Lina taught her three daughters how to make baskets and today both Maude Jones and Ida make good coiled baskets; Bessie Rogers, the oldest daughter, makes only cradleboards and twined baskets.

LINA IDITICAVA'S SKILL in making baskets is judged highly by her peers: "She makes very neat and pretty baskets. . . . The designs and sticks are all even

FIGURE 20. Ida, Lina, Maude, Belva (Toby's girl), July 1934.

37

... a very even and perfect edge ... fine weaving." Most of her baskets have eighteen or more stitches per inch and three of her best have counts of twenty-two and twenty-three stitches and nine coils per inch (no. 51, no. 53, no. 68). Even her baskets of average texture, such as no. 96 and no. 87, have beautifully regular work. A pinnacle of technical skill is reached in bowl no. 53. Sewing elements one thirty-second of an inch wide are placed very closely around coils an eighth of an inch in diameter. The unusual and exceedingly fine false braid or herringbone rim (fig. 21) is worked in black at twenty-two stitches to the inch. The only imperfection to be seen in this basket is the uneven spacing of some of the seven pairs of "ladders" ascending the walls.

Though the forms are flawlessly executed, Lina's baskets offer few surprises in size and shape. The favored circular plaques and trays, of nine to sixteen inches diameter, depart from normal in only one case: no. 83 has the exceptional

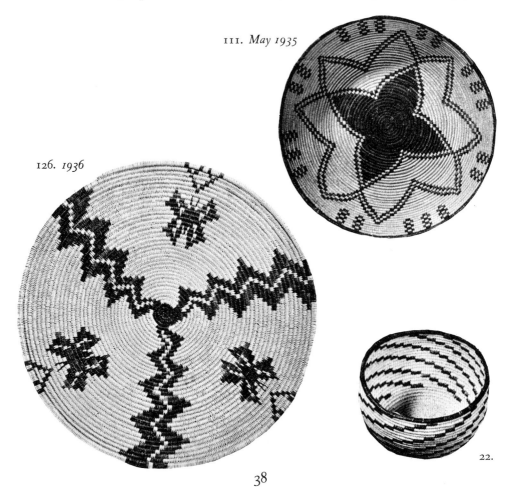

III. *May 1935*

126. *1936*

22.

38

depth of three inches. Globular or wide-mouthed bowls tend to be small, and these display the finest weaves.

Lina's geometric designs are near perfect and are more complex than those attempted by most other weavers: "She makes lots of designs in her work all the way through." Multiple encircling bands are favored, especially zigzag lines of bold or delicate proportions (no. 68, no. 83, no. 87, no. 100, no. 111). A distinctive motif is the band of pendant, curved triangles; some encircle a negative "star," "flower" or "leaf" motif (no. 68, no. 87, no. 95, no. 96, no. 100, no. 101). Centered motifs with a floral quality are used on many baskets (no. 95, no. 96, no. 111). The encircling bands on no. 51 and no. 68 (top) are among the oldest Supai designs and are used on many burden baskets and parching trays. Most of Lina's radiating patterns have excellent balance (no. 22, no. 91, no. 126), but one essay into isolated motifs, as yet unidentified, fared less well (no. 101).

53. *December 1932*

FIGURE 21. Detail of basket no. 53 showing herringbone rim.

51. *April 1935*

68. *June 1934*

95.

83. *June 1934*

87.

96.

91.

41

100.

116.

101.

KATIE MOONEY HAMIDREEK
1896–

Havasu Canyon was Katie Hamidreek's home for most of her life. She attended the day school there and later went to Phoenix for a year or so. Upon return to Supai she married Austin Hamidreek. (The old spelling of the name Hamidreek was *Hamtecq* meaning "nighthawk.") Austin and Katie Hamidreek lived at Grand Canyon in the 1930s where Austin worked for the Fred Harvey company. Katie made many baskets, some of excellent weave and construction, others coarse and rough. She sold all that she made and usually spent the money received at the general store in the village at Grand Canyon, buying sugar, flour, and some candy.

Katie always enjoyed making cradleboards. A miniature cradleboard ten inches long, made about 1935, was "for a doll." When Katie's eyesight began to fail, as she grew old, she continued to produce cradles, and this work gave her much satisfaction.

Katie's daughter, Gertrude Marshall, was inspired by her mother to try her hand at basketmaking, and recently has woven some nice baskets.

FIGURE 22. Katie Hamidreek and son, October 11, 1934.

43

THREE BASKETS SOLD to the McKees in 1933 and 1934 (no. 31, no. 82, no. 143) as well as a miniature cradleboard (no. 171) show Katie's skill and taste. Though forms, designs, and texture stay well within tradition, each basket is distinctive. One is a small plaque, the second a large tray, and the third a medium-sized bowl. They illustrate radiating and encircling geometrics, negative design, and various life forms. Two show fine coiling (no. 31, no. 143) and the other coarse (no. 82).

82. *October 1934*

A contrast of workmanship occurs within a single basket (no. 82) which begins and continues for twenty-four rounds in the finely-textured weave normal for Katie Hamidreek and then changes to grossly heavier coils (four per inch) and wider stitching (twelve per inch) for the remainder of the basket. The weaver herself offered no explanation, but the reader can speculate about ill health, a need to hurry, a change in available basketry materials, or an idle visiting basketmaker.

143. *August 1934*

31. *June 1933*

171. *Length 10″, width 4″*

ALICE WESCOGAME JONES
1892–1967

Alice Jones lived in Havasu Canyon much of her life, and attended school there. Later she married Alva Jones and went with him to live at Grand Canyon village where he was working. Alice would spend each winter at Grand Canyon, but always in March would return to her canyon home in order to plant her garden. She then would stay at Supai until cold weather put an end to farming.

Alice was a midwife and delivered many babies in Supai. She had eight children of her own, two of whom died in infancy. In spite of being a busy mother and midwife, Alice found time to make many baskets, including coiled pieces, burden baskets, cradleboards and water jars. Her weaving was fine and the designs traditional and attractive.

One of Alice's sons, Jack Jones, assisted Edwin McKee on several occasions as a packer during McKee's natural history and geological investigations in Grand Canyon. Her daughter, Elizabeth Jones Uqualla, has begun to weave baskets, thus carrying on a family tradition.

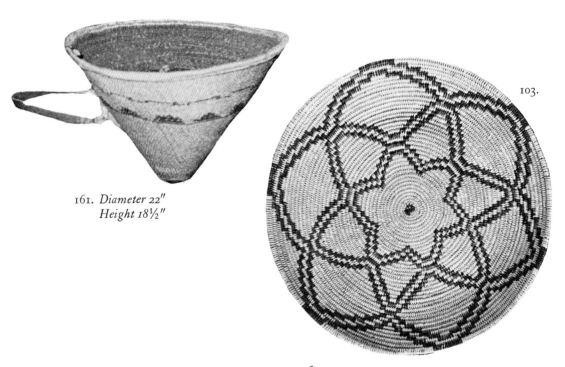

161. *Diameter 22"*
Height 18½"

103.

46

ALICE JONES' CIRCULAR, DEEP TRAY, no. 103, uses an early Havasupai design well known to many basketweaving peoples in the Southwest. A series of zigzag encircling bands or star-like designs abut, outer to inner points, thus forming a sort of diamond network over the entire surface. The light-dark contrast and the geometric balance of the pattern as developed by the weaver are quite pleasing.

174. *Diameter 17½"; 1938*

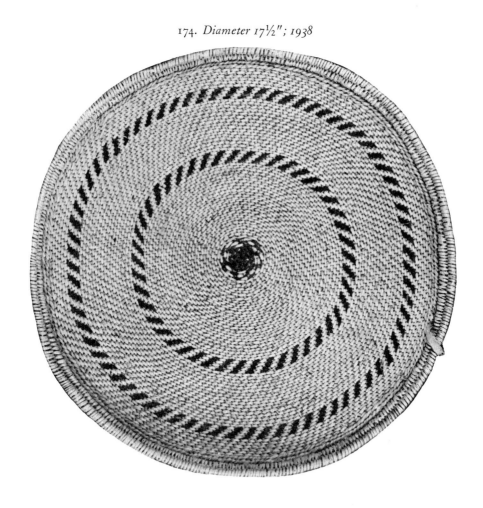

FAYE JONES MARSHALL (PAYA)
1912–1970

Faye Marshall lived in Havasu Canyon as a young girl. When she was eight years old she was sent away to school at Ft. Mohave, Arizona, and was there from 1920 to 1926. Instead of returning to Supai during summer vacation, she went to Pasadena, California, where she worked in various homes. After 1926 she continued her education in California, attending Sherman Institute at Riverside for a few years.

In 1930 Faye returned to Supai and married Gilbert Marshall. He worked at Grand Canyon much of the time, so he and his family then lived on the South Rim. In later years Faye was married to Lemuel Paya. Faye was an excellent basketmaker and some of the best coiled baskets in the collection are her work.

About 1968 the McKees happened to meet Faye at the head of the Hualapai trail. During their conversation that day, Faye mentioned that she was trying to arouse interest in basketmaking among the young Supai girls and had begun a small class in which she was attempting to teach several of the girls. Unfortunately, ill health put an end to this project, and in spite of care at the hospital in Phoenix, Faye died in 1970.

FIGURE 23. Faye Marshall (Paya), center, with party at Hualapai Hilltop, 1968.

TWO OF FAYE'S BASKETS rank as outstanding. A circular bowl with recurved rim (no. 54) is exceedingly well shaped and fine-textured with twenty-two stitches and ten coils per inch. The other plaque (no. 139) features an extremely well planned and executed design of fine central spirals enclosed in a large-scale "leaf" band. Indeed, all of her baskets have beautifully worked out traditional geometric designs.

Tray no. 109 has a strange dual character: the initial five rounds and the outer third of the basket display close, even stitching, but the area between has coarse, irregular texture. Did an expert basketmaker begin, then turn over the work to a beginner or poor basketmaker, only to resume work herself for a better completion?

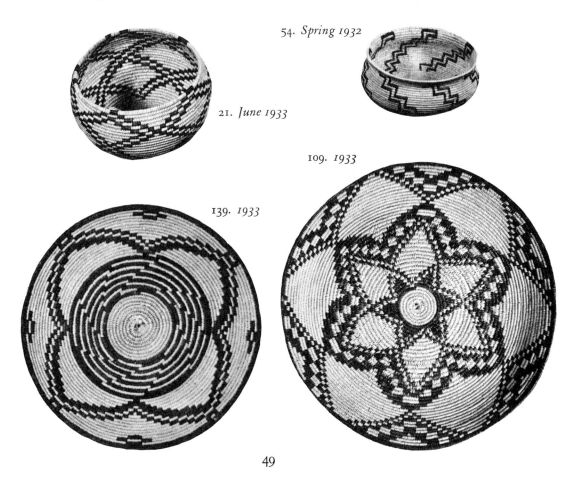

54. *Spring 1932*

21. *June 1933*

109. *1933*

139. *1933*

49

ELSIE SPOONHEAD SINYELLA
1910–

Elsie Sinyella spent an uneventful childhood in Havasu Canyon where she attended the local day school. Later she went to school in Albuquerque, New Mexico, and after that spent some time working in homes in California. Following her return to Arizona, she married West Sinyella: they lived part time in Supai and other times at the Grand Canyon. Periodically West was employed by the National Park Service.

Elsie's baskets, collected at Grand Canyon in the 1930s, shows a variety of workmanship. Later she lost interest in basketmaking and made none for many years. But in 1970, when she was urged by the storekeeper at Peach Springs to begin again, she produced some fine coiled pieces (Bateman, 1972, p. 75). She has also worked on twined baskets, but ill health has forced her to stop.

49.

29. *October 1934*

ELSIE SINYELLA SPECIALIZED in circular bowls, especially low and wide-mouthed types with curving walls. The board range of workmanship possible from even a single weaver is well illustrated in two bowls sold to the McKees by Elsie in October 1934: no. 29 is extra large, with very coarse texture (5½ coils, 15 stitches per inch), and irregular work; whereas no. 38, the smallest bowl in the collection, has exceptionally fine texture (ten coils, twenty stitches per inch).

Another basketmaker stated that Elsie Sinyella did not use much black, and, indeed, the black designs on these baskets are sparse and mostly small. Some of her bowls have designs on the bottom. Bird motifs are featured on all baskets in the collection.

33. *April 1935*

38. *(not to scale)*

38. *October 1934*

MABEL TOUP BARNEY (also called Stella Barney)
1885–1945

Mabel Barney lived at the Supai camp near Grand Canyon village in the 1930s. To earn money she made and sold coiled baskets. Although Mabel was handicapped by a paralyzed arm and was blind in one eye, she made surprisingly good baskets. Sometimes her husband, Supai Barney, would help her.

In making her baskets Mabel would clamp the basket between her knees and use her good hand to drive the awl and weaving splints through. Because of her handicap, the baskets were of a rather loose, irregular weave and the pattern somewhat unbalanced. The designs in Mabel's baskets are unusual; she commonly used animal motifs (dog or horse, no. 106; bat, no. 121) and other objects such as a corn plant (no. 160) and trail (no. 106). An interesting geometric motif is the ticked three-line figure in small scale around the center of no. 182 and enlarged around no. 108's center.

Other Supai basketmakers are generally so taken with these unusual "good" and "very pretty" designs that they judge very leniently the "not so straight" patterns and "not so tight" weave of this distinctive basketmaker.

FIGURE 24. Mabel Barney, Grand Canyon, 1938. Her Hualapai friend (left) did not wish to have her picture taken.

FOUR OF MABEL'S BASKETS evidently were started by some skilled friend who worked the initial eight to eleven rounds in close, fairly even stitches, seventeen to twenty-one to the inch. At the transition to design (see no. 97, no. 182, no. 106) or at the break from center design (no. 121), the weaving becomes distinctly more coarse, irregular, and loose. Presumably this is Mabel Barney's own work, with four to six coils and fourteen to seventeen stitches per inch. However, tray no. 108 is puzzling, for it shows in its entirety very close and even work. Made late in the period, it may be evidence of a major triumph over handicaps by the basketmaker.

A trademark of Mabel's baskets is a skewing of pattern, resulting from her impaired vision. Balance is invariably off, as in the irregular spacing of the radiating motifs in no. 106, no. 108, no. 121, and no. 182.

Only very shallow trays and plaques of average size were made by Mabel, as might be expected. The oval plaque, no. 106, is unique in its narrowness, as well as in its centered, asymmetrical design layout. The tripartite layout in no. 121 and no. 106 is uncommon in Supai baskets.

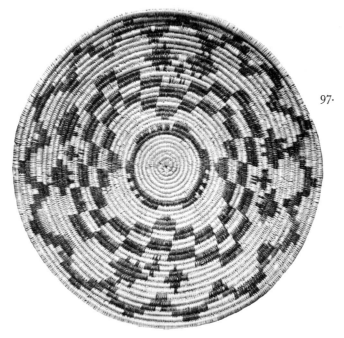

97.

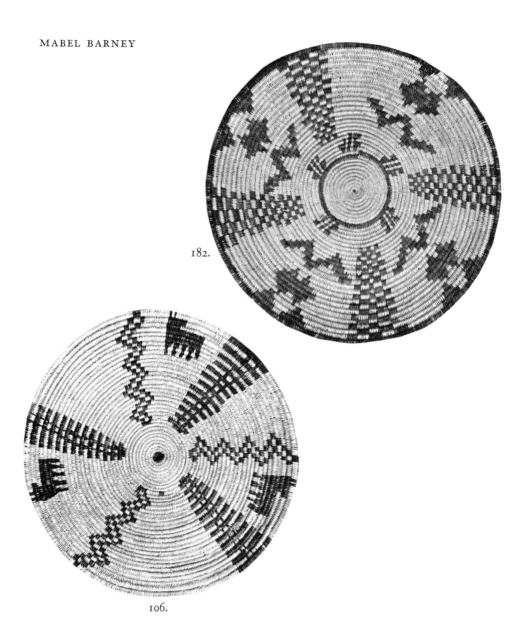

182.

106.

108. *June 1938*

121.

106. *February 1934*

TEYAVA [LAME] JONES JACK
1877–1941

When Teyava Jack came to Grand Canyon village to sell her baskets in the 1930s, she always put on her best clothes and carried her wares in a large cotton flour sack. She was a shy but friendly woman. She was then called "Susie," but it has since been learned that "the English name 'Susie' was a casual name given by whites to nearly all the women."

In 1933 Susie made a basket of unusual shape—a bowl on a pedestal—which is unique in the collection. The swastika on this basket (no. 11) is one of the few in this collection, although the symbol is very ancient and has been used by early people in many parts of the world. Other designs on her baskets were geometric and well planned, but her weave was coarse.

FIGURE 25. Teyava Jones Jack, Grand Canyon, March 1936.

SUSIE JACK'S TWO MEDIUM-SIZED, shallow trays typify Havasupai basketry in technical as well as in design features. Tray no. 117 is excellent in its near perfection of balance, achieved by careful placement of dark triangles in both inner and outer pattern bands.

Her pedestal bowl (no. 11) probably imitates a non-Indian compote dish. It consists of a shallow, straight-sided, flat-bottomed bowl—complete in itself—sitting atop a short neck that curves abruptly to a broad foot. The inside of the bowl is the work surface and was made in opposition to the normal, easiest procedure. The resulting coarse and irregular texture, however, hardly detracts from the technical feat represented by this basket. The weaver seems to have been so preoccupied with form that pattern was little developed: a four-point, narrow line zigzag encircles the bowl from pedestal to rim, and swastika and diamond motifs are spotted on foot and wall.

11. *1933*

120. *May 1933*

166. *Diameter 9⅞"*
Height 10½

117. *February 1936*

ORA SINYELLA UQUALLA (Watahomigie)
1914–1973

Ora Uqualla lived at Grand Canyon village in the 1930s where she often worked in the homes of National Park Service families. Her first husband was Harlow Uqualla. Later she married Phillip Watahomigie. Although not a prolific basketmaker, Ora made typical Supai baskets, only one of which is represented in this collection of the 1930s.

THE SINGLE BASKET (no. 23) identified as Ora Uqualla's in this collection is an open-mouthed bowl with a vase-like shape and an unusually tapered lower section. The workmanship is good but the design is atypical. The complex primary motif used by Ora has four expanding tiers of opposed hooked lines, rising above a common basal line. To a non-Indian eye, deer antlers may be suggested. More interesting, however, is the interpretation given by another Supai: "devil's claws," i.e., the seed pod of *Proboscidea sp.* from whose tough covering the black designs in this basketry are made. Eagles and arrowheads are said to have been used by Ora on other baskets.

23.

MAE CLINTON TILOUSI
1905–

When she was a young girl Mae Tilousi became interested in making baskets. Lilly Burro and Yewaia Paketekopa showed her how to collect and prepare weaving materials and how to weave both coiled and twined baskets.

After marrying Paul Tilousi, Mae moved to Grand Canyon village where Paul was working for the National Park Service and later for Kolb's Studio. In succeeding years the Tilousi family moved about in northern Arizona and lived wherever Paul could find work. During this time Mae continued her basket-making and sold her pieces to tourists, curio stores and even to other Supais.

Three of Mae Tilousi's baskets were obtained by the McKees when she called at their back door in the middle 1930s. Two were so small as to be almost miniatures. These were very finely woven, in keeping with the small size of the plaques. A larger plaque was woven with coarser texture and a bold design.

Today, as an old woman, Mae is still actively making twined ware. She recently has completed several twined baskets, including unpitched water jars, trays, burden baskets, and bowls. She also makes cradleboards for Supai mothers to use.

FIGURE 26. Mae Tilousi with her recent twined baskets, April 1974.

59

THE SMALLEST PLAQUE in the McKee collection, no. 144, was woven by Mae Tilousi. It measures 5¾ inches in diameter and has very fine texture.

The design style of bowl no. 26 and plaque no. 144 is spare and simple. A few geometric motifs, mostly in oblique pairs, have been placed midway in the design field and are unaccompanied by any other pattern. Mae explained recently that when she made these particular baskets she knew few designs; later she learned to make many more. Mae's stated preference in design, however, is the simple style used in twined ware. She feels that some weavers put in too

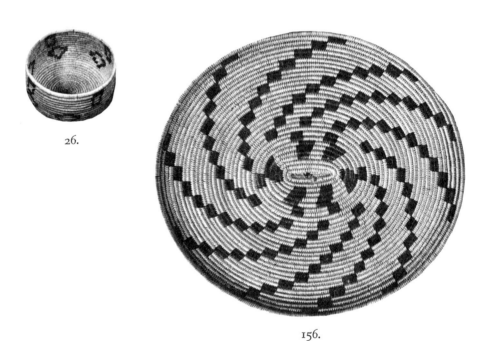

26.

156.

many designs, possibly because they have an abundance of devil's claw and like working with it.

There is much black in plaque no. 132, but the design, which Mae likened to a flower in a memorial wreath, is still simple. The spiralling pattern of plaque no. 156 is more complex. This basket shows the close and regular weave that Mae was capable of doing.

Mae does not apply names to her own designs, nor does she attempt to identify the designs of others, stating that "it is up to the maker as to what it is."

132.

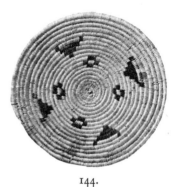

144.

CLARA SPOONHEAD WESCOGAME
1904– between 1935–40

Clara Wescogame spent most of her life in Havasu Canyon. She received her schooling at the day school there. In later years, during the 1930s, she lived at the Grand Canyon, where her husband, Bela Wescogame, was employed.

As a young girl Clara learned from her mother, Susie Spoonhead, how to weave coiled baskets, and preferred to weave bowls rather than plaques. Her baskets were of typical Supai style, but her designs were quite distinctive.

A HIGHLY INDIVIDUAL APPROACH is shown on the two baskets obtained from Clara Wescogame. On both of these the form is a circular, flat-bottomed bowl, more straight-sided and deeper than is normal for Supai bowls. A blocky pattern of four massive vertical motifs compliments well the high walls and large size of basket no. 10. In basket no. 34 vertical and encircling checkerboard bands form framing lines around the two large eagles which are the principal motifs. Such checkerboard frames have seldom been used by other Supai women.

34. *August 1933*

10.

62

MINNIE WESCOGAME MARSHALL

1920–

As a little girl Minnie Marshall watched her mother, Clara Wescogame, and her grandmother, Susie Spoonhead, make baskets. When she went to school at Valentine, Arizona, she was taught how to start a basket and in 1935, at the age of fifteen, she made her first one. It was a plaque about five inches across. She recalls, "It wasn't so good, but they put it in an exhibit." It was not until she returned to Supai to get married that she made another basket, a tiny one about an inch and a half across, which she sold for fifty cents. She has continued to make baskets and some are fine, coiled work.

In 1968 when the McKees were in Supai on a trip they stopped to visit with Minnie. She proudly showed them a pair of mountain sheep horns which were rather smelly as the flesh had not been cleaned from them. Minnie told how she had grabbed her husband's gun when she saw the mountain sheep on the cliffs above her house and shot the animal, felling it with one blast. This was a remarkable feat since she had never shot a gun before. She was anxious for Mr. McKee to take the horns "for the museum."

FIGURE 27. Minnie Marshall and her recent baskets, April 1974.

63

MINNIE MARSHALL'S CIRCULAR TRAYS made in the thirties range widely from large and coarse (no. 78, with thirteen stitches and four coils per inch) to small and fine (no. 112, with twenty-three stitches and nine coils per inch). The latter very fine basket took over a month to make. Minnie says that its bands make a pretty design but don't mean anything. The outer band of enclosed oblique lines is an old design used on twined utility ware (compare with Lina Iditicava, no. 68 and no. 51).

Although her baskets contrast strongly in shape with the bowls of her mother, Clara Wescogame, there is great similarity in boldness of pattern. Eagles, similar but not identical, were used by both women, and Minnie Marshall continues to make them though she no longer puts in the legs, so prominent in no. 89.

89.

78.

112.

MARY BURRO WESCOGAME
1866–1953

"Supai Mary" was one of the elderly Supai women living at the Grand Canyon off and on during the 1930's. More often she could be found in Supai village in Havasu Canyon tending her garden. Mary was a famous horsewoman in the early days. Even in the 1920s and 30s, when she was nearly sixty years or older, she won many horse races at the annual 4th of July rodeos held in Flagstaff and Grand Canyon. While Mary was not an expert basketmaker, she did make a few trays rather crude in design and construction.

FIGURE 28. Mary Wescogame "relaxing" near the trail, Supai, May 1936.

FIGURE 29. Mary Wescogame with daughter Viola (Crook), aged 17, Supai, June 1929.

MARY'S BASKET, no. 107, contains all the traditional elements of form, construction, and design, but the workmanship is inexpert. Her greatest contribution in basketry surely was through her daughters, Viola and Ethel, who became expert weavers by watching and learning from their mother and her friends.

107. *April 1932*

ETHEL WESCOGAME JACK
1908–

For many years Ethel Jack lived at the Grand Canyon where she worked for the Fred Harvey company and later at the Kolb Studio.

As a school girl Ethel once spent the summer working in the home of a California family. These people were interested in their Indian helper and took her on a boat trip from Los Angeles to Catalina Island. This was an experience Ethel never forgot and later, when she returned to Arizona and was making coiled baskets in order to earn extra money, she made a basket in the shape of a boat (no. 58). This uniquely-shaped basket with a keel and a prow, as well as a "water line" in the design, puzzled other Supais. Upon seeing the basket, one friend asked, "What is the matter with this?"

In 1972 Ethel returned to Supai to live permanently near her sister, Viola Crook. She seldom makes coiled baskets now, but concentrates instead on twined ones and cradleboards.

FIGURE 30. Ethel Jack at Grand Canyon village, August 1937.

FIGURE 31. Ethel Jack in Supai, May 1973.

68

THE BASKETS OF THIS WEAVER form quite a distinctive group in form and design. Instead of the typical circular tray, she made many oval plaques of medium size. One (no. 159) is unusually long and narrow with slightly up-turned edges. Her small circular bowls have a variety of wall and rim shapes.

Many of Ethel Jack's designs are highly imaginative. Some are unique, but others are ancient motifs used in new ways. Her own comments, made in 1973, best describe these designs. Bowl no. 45: "Broken rocks at the Canyon. Each time I look at it, it reminds me of rocks. I worked right there at the Canyon." Bowl no. 40: "Chopping wood." She explained that the horizontal line and the upstanding ends are the log, whereas the small motif in the center of the "log" is a chicken. Bowl no. 43 and plaque no. 159, made during the winter, have similar opposed, curving, hook-like motifs, about which the weaver could not remember anything. Other motifs of no. 159 include "Up and down hills on the edge, and the two long lines are the hills." This plaque and the other (no. 150) display a reverse imagery that is highly unusual in Supai basketry.

Ethel described plaque no. 150 as follows: "I wanted the center to be something like a lizard; then I changed my mind and put out arms. The outside was going to be like a railroad track and just stopped there." (The rim differs on one end, indicating a premature finishing for the basket.) About plaque no. 155 she says: "Center looks like a lizard—crazy!" She was inspired by the work of her friend Dottie Watahomigie, known for her many lizard designs.

The remarkable basket no. 58, referred to before, which was modelled after a boat, deserves detailed analysis. It has a recurved base with a long, narrow, half-inch high flat-bottomed section that represents a keel and curves abruptly into the main elongated globular body of the "boat." At one end is a prow, built up of three tapered coils added in black at the rim. A "waterline" in the design gives a final nautical touch.

Although imaginative designs are her forte, Ethel Jack produced well-made baskets. Her finest, no. 159, has twenty-three stitches and eight coils per inch.

155.

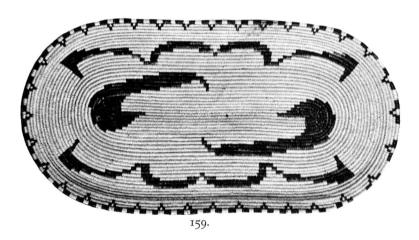

159.

45. *March 1935*

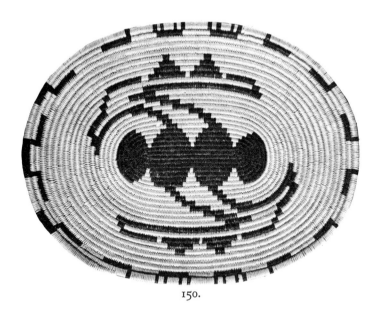

150.

40. *April 1938*

58. *April 1935*

43.

VIOLA WESCOGAME CROOK

1912–

Viola Crook, daughter of Mary Wescogame, far surpassed her mother in basketry. She began to weave baskets while in her teens and made many during her placid life in Havasu Canyon. Viola's designs are bold and well executed. When she sent several of her baskets to the Arizona State Fair she received prizes for them, including one first, a second, and a third prize.

FIGURE 32. Viola Crook and daughter Hazel, South Rim, Grand Canyon, March 1937.

FIGURE 33. Viola Crook with basket at Grand Canyon, August 1937.

BOWLS MADE BY VIOLA CROOK during the 1930s are pleasing in their crisp symmetry and traditional styling. The small bowl, no. 20, woven when she was but sixteen years old and shyly brought for sale in the company of her mother, shows a beginner's simple design and coarse texture. Her craftsmanship developed greatly over the years culminating in the complex realistic design and perfect balance of bowl no. 71, with its fine texture and twenty-four stitches per inch.

Viola's favored oval forms have bases and little curve in the low walls. Blocks of geometric or realistic design are symmetrically placed at each end and different ones are along the sides. Her animal forms, especially the butterfly, have fine detail. In no. 63 she made two forms of eagle, one in solid black with legs below outspread wings and the other in "stippled" black with legs under the tail. This unusual stippling effect, produced by alternating black and plain stitches in each row of design, also is employed quite effectively, in bowl no. 61.

Like the designs of her sister, Ethel Jack, Viola's designs have great flair—but within a more restrained traditional framework. Because Viola declines to make comment on her own baskets, we do not know whether her designs also are based on a vivid personal imagery.

61. *August 1937*

20. *June 1929*

63. *February 1933*

71.

73

MECCA MULGULO UQUALLA

1905–

As a child Mecca Uqualla went to the "Old School" in Supai village. This institution required its students to dress in uniforms and to wear high laced shoes, a practice which all the children hated.

Mecca was quite young when she married Toby Uqualla, a very industrious young man who raised cattle on the plateau above Havasu Canyon. During the 1930s when the McKees were collecting Havasupai baskets, Toby had the job of hauling mail into and out of Havasu Canyon from Grand Canyon village. In those days he had to drive his truck some thirty miles over an exceedingly rough road to the head of the Topocoba Trail and then use horses for the final twelve miles down to Supai village. Toby was the last mail-carrier to use this route; now an easier road and trail are followed from Peach Springs.

Mecca made many coiled baskets when she was a young woman, all of which she sold. In her later years she has continued to weave baskets, mostly trays and bowls, but keeps them for use in her own home near the center of the village. She has always liked using designs of butterflies and lizards.

FIGURE 34. Mecca Uqualla and her recent baskets, April 1974.

A SINGLE BASKET in the collection attributed to Mecca (no. 8) must be described in superlatives. It is the largest bowl in the collection and features very heavy, yet evenly sewn coils. The leaf motifs are made with a realism unusual for Supai basketry. Some contemporary basketmakers feel this extraordinary design is traditional, but others term it "not Indian."

8.

STELLA TEYACH KCHAVA [Corn Eater] YUNOSI
1887–1950

Stella Yunosi lived most of her life in her native Havasu Canyon home and was educated the the school nearby. She was married first to Chief Jasper Manakaja, who was the father of her daughter, Edith, a future fine basketmaker like her mother. Manakaja was formerly written *Hamána Kejáa* which means "Who cares for his children." He was head chief of the Havasupai from 1900 to 1942. He died at the age of ninety-two in February 1942. Stella's second husband, Yunosi (a medicine man), provided her with a unique checkerboard design which she used in several of her baskets.

Stella was one of those individuals who was always busy. Each day after working in her fields and looking after the welfare of her family, she would characteristically settle down to making baskets.

Stella was a very prolific basketmaker and her excellent productions brought her much ready cash. On her frequent visits to Grand Canyon village during the 1930s she sold her baskets not only to the McKees, but also to the manager of the Hopi House and to tourists along the rim walk.

FIGURE 35. Stella Yunosi displays newly-made plaques near McKee home at Grand Canyon, January 1936.

76

STELLA YUNOSI FAVORED unusually large oval and circular trays. The largest basket in the collection, no. 77, was made by her. This tray measures 22 inches across and 3¼ inches high, and has thick walls forming an unusual, very shallow cone shape of massive proportions. Almost as large are plaques no. 122 and no. 145 and shallow tray no. 146. These large baskets sold for about fifteen dollars each in the 1930s. Stella also produced some extra-small trays (no. 113, no. 114, no. 118).

Stella Yunosi's trays exhibit a great variety of shapes: flat-bottomed with straight walls, either short or widely splayed; gradually curving from center to rim; and shallowly conical. Her skill in creating form shows itself most clearly in bowl no. 52 and in jars no. 3, no. 4, and no. 5. The jar form in no. 4, technically difficult to weave, was made even more difficult by the inclusion of a sharp curve on the shoulder.

Stella's baskets are evenly, but not finely textured with few exceptions. The largest trays and jars use extra-heavy twigs in the foundation, so that coils number only four or five per inch. In all the baskets, stitches tend to be spaced widely, running about fifteen to seventeen per inch. Several examples show

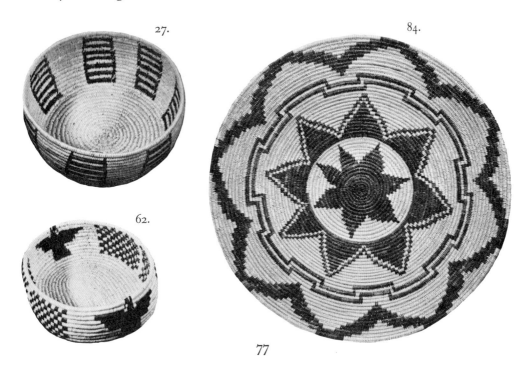

27.

84.

62.

Stella's capability for doing exceedingly fine work, with as many as 23 stitches and 9½ coils per inch (no. 52, no. 113, no. 118).

Stella Yunosi's designs have great distinction in both concept and execution. Her usual bold geometric designs complement well the broad surface of the large baskets, and when more delicate motifs are used, their repetition adds needed weight (no. 52, no. 90). Linear radiating patterns described by Supai weavers as "ladders" (no. 27 and no. 122), "trails" (no. 105), "trees" (no. 52), and "arrowheads" (no. 2 and no. 90) occur in many places. Encircling bands form themes (no. 84, no. 123) and in other designs combine with individual block motifs (no. 113, no. 145, no. 146). A framing line used in many baskets is called "corral" or "fence" (no. 84, no. 90, no. 113, no. 146). A spiralling stepped line is used so densely in two baskets that its effect is that of an overall pattern (no. 118, no. 148).

Many of Stella Yunosi's designs were quite individualistic. Her distinctive elongated, double-centered boxes, arranged in various ways, are called "boxes" by other basket weavers (no. 3, no. 145, no. 146). In one basket, however, they

145. *January 1936*

form an object that has been identified as a *cathok,* the conical Havasupai burden basket (no. 145, central end motifs). The rarely-used cross occurs in no. 146. The few times Stella depicted plant or animal forms, she employed her own type of stylization (roadrunner in no. 114, eagle in no. 113) or abstraction (leaves in two encircling bands in no. 123 and different, flat leaves in no. 77).

One of the most interesting designs on baskets in this collection was used exclusively by Stella. This design occurs on a tall jar (no. 4) and in a large plaque (no. 99). Its origin in 1934, referred to earlier, was recently described by her daughter, Edith Putesoy: "Her husband, Yunosi, was a medicine man. He dreamed about it. He made it on a paper and she copied it on the baskets." Here, then, is a true "dream design," but one with no symbolic content at all, according to Edith. Even in this case of specific artistic inspiration (rare in accounts of North American Indian art), the basketmaker has expressed her own artistic license in executing the design, for the two baskets differ: the jar has small checkerboards within a large checkerboard, whereas the plaque achieved the same effect with small stepped lines within large stepped (spiralling) lines.

146.

177. 1936

122. *January 1936*

176. 1936

2.

82

5.

4. *August 1934*

118.

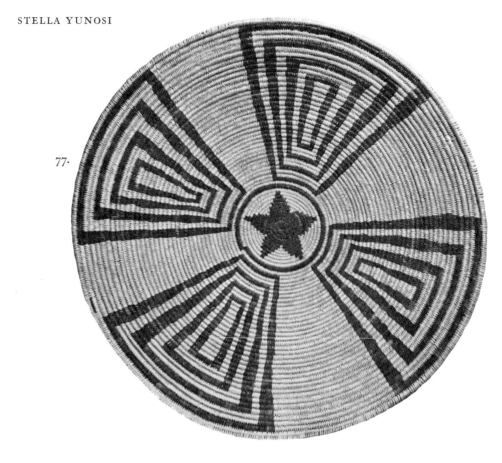

77.

114.

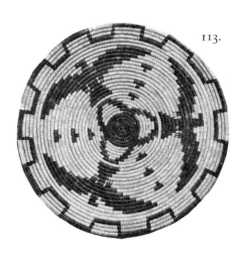

113.

151.

52.

90.

123. *April 1934*

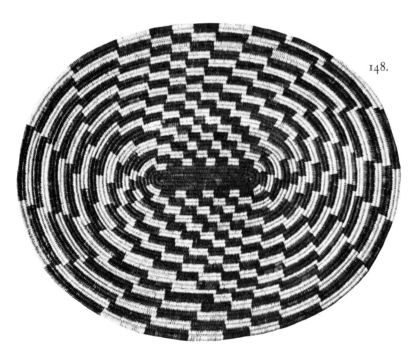

148.

105.

99.

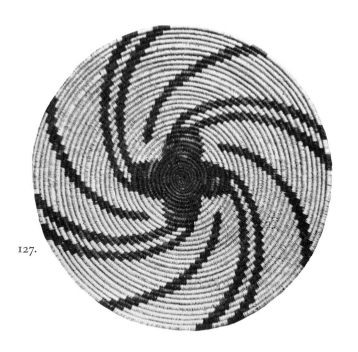

127.

3.

EDITH MANAKAJA PUTESOY
1909–

Edith Putesoy's early childhood was spent in Havasu Canyon where she had her first schooling. In 1920 she was sent to Ft. Mohave Indian School in western Arizona. In the summer each year she went to Pasadena, California, to work in private homes. In 1926 she attended Sherman Institute in Riverside, California, for one and a half years. Upon her return to Supai in 1928 she married Mack Putesoy. In the 1930s they lived at Grand Canyon where Mack was working for the National Park Service. In spite of having the care of a large family and periodically doing housework in the homes of local residents, Edith found time to make many excellent baskets which she sold at the local stores and to private individuals. When many Havasupai women gave up making baskets in the

FIGURE 36. Edith Putesoy with husband Mack and baby, November 1934.

FIGURE 37. Edith Putesoy with cradleboard and plaque at Grand Canyon, 1937.

1940s, Edith and her mother, Stella Yunosi, continued to weave them. In 1954 Edith demonstrated basketmaking at the Heard Museum and at the Arizona State Fair in Phoenix. She was paid twelve dollars a day at the State Fair. In addition to the money she earned, she received several ribbons for her baskets. Many of her baskets also were sold at the Heard Museum.

One unique plaque (no. 124) made by Edith has as its design the profile of a man with feathers in his hair and a sparse beard. When questioned in 1971 about this basket Edith said, "I made it because I thought it would be funny."

Edith is still making baskets in 1974. She enjoys this occupation and says, "Every morning I get up and work on it. I really enjoy it. Sometimes I let several days go by and am too lazy to work on baskets, but then I go back to it."

FIGURE 38. Edith Putesoy in Havasu Canyon, May 1973.

THE FINE BASKETMAKING of Stella Yunosi continued in the work of her daughter, Edith Putesoy. The same mastery of form and pattern, together with perhaps even greater technical skill and different designs combine to produce the unique style of Edith's basketry.

Plaques and trays with low, curving walls are typically medium-large. Equal emphasis goes to bowls, which display great diversity of size and shape: flat, curved, and footed bases; globular and flaring walls; straight and recurved rims; circular and elliptical shapes, the latter in her largest bowls. Edith called the unusual double bowl form (no. 13, no. 14) an old shape, and explained that such bowls were used for holding fruit or corn. Although she made the jar form, none are in this collection.

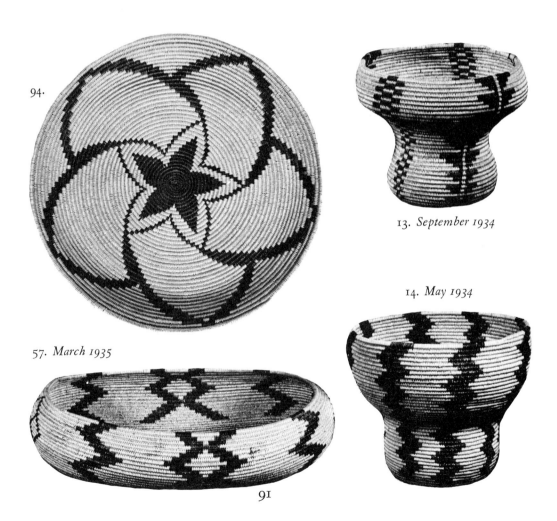

94.

13. *September 1934*

14. *May 1934*

57. *March 1935*

Almost all of Edith's work is closely and regularly stitched and evenly coiled, more so than her mother's work. Fineness differs greatly, from twelve to twenty-three stitches and four to ten coils per inch, depending largely on the size of the basket. Her finest weaving in a small bowl (no. 44) and in a tray (no. 141) compares closely to her mother's finest, but Edith has done more of such work than Stella did.

A general fineness of line and balance pervades Edith's designs and the planning and execution of pattern are unexcelled by any weaver. Spiralling patterns are her specialty, using the "wind" motif (no. 19, no. 44, no. 80, no. 93,

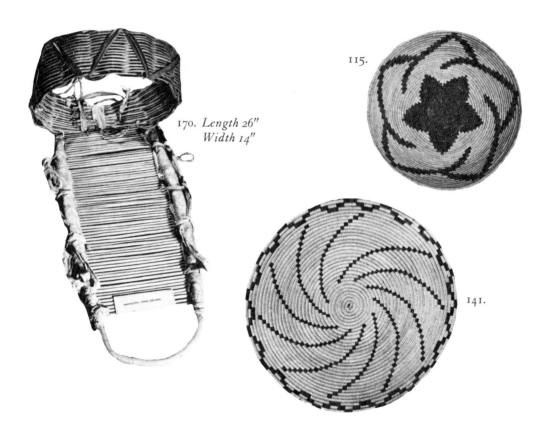

170. *Length 26"*
Width 14"

115.

141.

no. 119, no. 128, no. 141, no. 175), "leaves" (no. 85, no. 94, no. 115, no. 129, no. 137), or "lightning" (no. 42, no. 130). Linear motifs occur vertically on double and ellipsoidal bowls and appear as "trees" (no. 13, no. 56), objects "like arrowheads" (no. 13), and "lightning" (no. 14, no. 57). Dark bands with negative design motifs that she uses are distinctive (no. 18, no. 46, no. 85, no. 110). Although she uses plants and animals infrequently, bowl no. 37 features ducks amid cattails.

Edith Putesoy's skill extends to all types of basketry, including burden baskets and parching trays. One of her cradleboards is shown in no. 170.

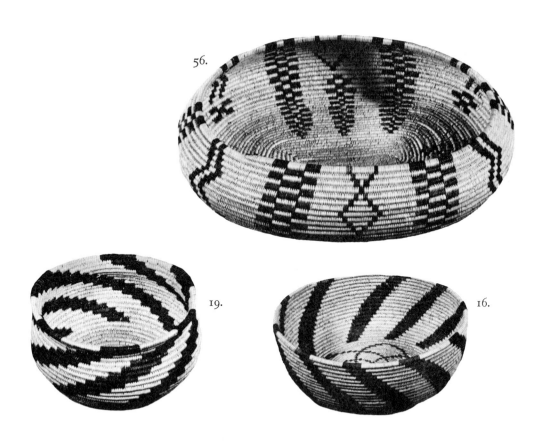

56.

19.

16.

110.

46. *July 1934*

124. *March 1935*

137.

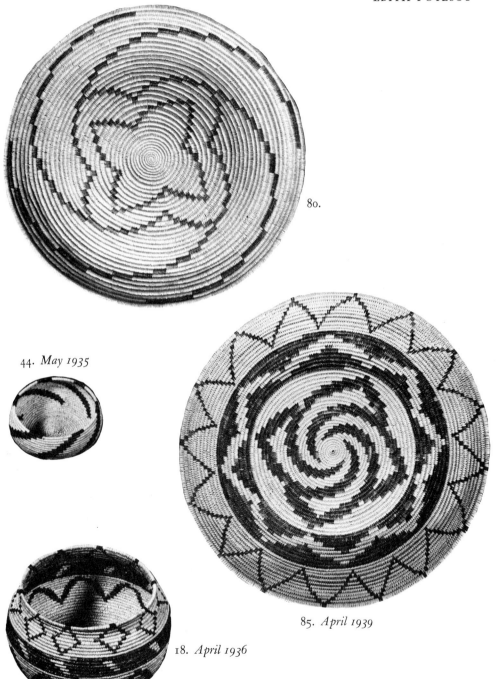

80.

44. *May 1935*

85. *April 1939*

18. *April 1936*

128.

93.

130. *January 1936*

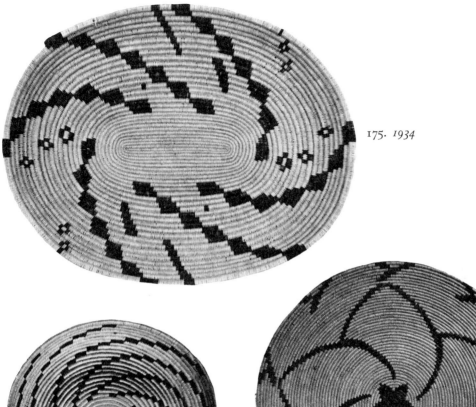

175. *1934*

119.

129. *November 1934*

42.

37. *June 1939*

48. *May 1935*

NINA STARKEY SIYUJA
1879–1934

Nina Siyuja produced some of the finest baskets made in the 1930s. She was a Hualapai from Seligman, Arizona, and her schooling was at the Indian school at Valentine. After marrying Richard Siyuja, a Havasuapi, she lived in Havasu Canyon and at the Grand Canyon where she learned how to make baskets from Havasupai women friends. She made coiled baskets only, and became very proficient in weaving bowls and trays of all sizes. She produced baskets until her death in 1934.

For many years her daughter, Virginia Hanna, has been postmistress at the United States post office in Supai. Virginia never has found time to try her hand at basketmaking.

32. *March 1932*

153.

55. *1932*

NONE OF THE BASKETS OBTAINED from Nina Siyuja can be termed "ordinary," for she commonly employed some trick of design. For example, she made two oval plaques that are nearly identical in size, shape and rim treatment. In design, both have the same central serrated motif bordered by two outer bands, but the treatment is so different that each basket is quite distinctive.

In plaque no. 138 the multiple centered "flower" or "leaves" is transformed from the usual by a flourish of out-of scale radiating arms. An atypical mixture of birds on bowl no. 32 shows ducks and eagles together. Several Havasupai basketmakers have been questioned about the unusual paired motifs on bowl no. 55, but as yet no one has been able to identify them.

The small bowl, no. 55, is also nearly flawless in its technical aspects. Ten coils to the inch are sewn evenly with twenty stitches along each inch, and there is absolute symmetry of design. It is undoubtedly one of the finest baskets in the collection.

138.

152.

EUNICE TAHUTA JONES
1876–1964

Eunice Tahuta (meaning Hidden) Jones lived in Havasu Canyon all her life. Her father was said to have been Wa-sti-kema who was also the father of Chief Manakaja. Eunice was the wife of Joe Jones.

Eunice is represented in the collection by only one basket, a large oval bowl (no. 70) made when she was fifty-three years old. Its form, design, and weave are typical of Havasupai work in all except one respect, that is, the little-used ticked rim, form of alternate plain and black stitches.

70. *June 1929*

SWEJAKEJA KWAK KETA WATAHOMIGIE
1864– date of death unknown

Susie, as Swejakeja was commonly called, was an infrequent visitor to Grand Canyon village in the 1930s. When she came it was usually to visit her son, Elmer, who was working for the National Park Service as a day laborer at that time. She was half Hualapai because her father, Kwak keta [Elk] was a Hualapai. Susie was not a prolific basketmaker and only one of her trays is found in the collection.

AN INTERESTING TYPE OF BASKET (no. 104) made by Susie in the spring of 1933, is a circular tray with slightly upturned edges. This basket has the much-used center and banded pattern, to which foreign color elements were added. The two enclosing fret lines were dyed black, although they are now faded to a purplish grey. The center part was dyed a bright gold, but is now faded to an orange tone. Such dyed colors, although common in Hualapai baskets, were seldom used by the Havasupais and then only by the very old women, according to one of the modern basketmakers. Apparently, therefore, Susie Watahomigie when she made this basket used an old technique known to few Supais or one she learned from her Hualapai relatives.

104. *May 1933*

EFFIE MEXICAN JACK HANNA
1908–

Effie Hanna was born at Supai in 1908, but has lived most of her life outside the canyon. She went to California as a school girl and stayed there ten years, almost forgetting the Supai language during that time. In 1928 she moved to Grand Canyon village where her husband, Henry Hanna, worked for the National Park Service. She was employed at various times by the Fred Harvey company, the Santa Fe railroad, and the McKee family. Effie and Henry had five sons, of whom two have survived and live at Supai. Widowed since 1971, she has lived mostly at Peach Springs in recent years, but hopes to go "home" to Supai to live permanently.

FIGURE 39. Effie Hanna with her first basket, May 1936.

EFFIE HANNA'S PLAQUE no. 131 has a story: it is the only basket she ever made. She learned by watching her cousin, Edith Putesoy, who started this basket and helped her with it. The design was Effie's own (but compare it with Edith's no. 130). She started to make the Bright Angel trail on it, but did not finish because "it ended up looking like a vulture or something." She brought this first effort to the McKee home in May 1936, justifiably proud, for its weave is very close and even.

131. *May 1936*

DOTTIE CROZIER WATAHOMIGIE
1883–1937

Dottie Watahomigie was a Hualapai and secured her schooling at the Valentine Indian school. She married Flynn Watahomigie, a Havasupai, and they took up residence at Supai and at Grand Canyon village. Dottie learned to make excellent baskets and produced many of various shapes and sizes. She delighted in using unusual designs of animals and plants which other women later copied. According to Edith Putesoy, Dottie sometimes used dye "because she was a Hualapai."

81.

DOTTIE WATAHOMIGIE'S BASKETS show great versatility in form, including not only the usual circular or oval, shallow bowl and tray forms, but also the rare double-bowl form (no. 12 and no. 15). Specimen no. 15 is one of the finest examples of the double-bowl form, with subtle curves, perfect balance, and a well-coordinated network design.

Although her workmanship generally is of average quality, Dottie Wata-homigie wove some exceptionally fine-textured, close, even baskets, as illustrated by no. 36 and no. 158. Both of these have eight coils and twenty to twenty-one stitches to the inch.

This basketmaker was well known for her unusual animal designs. In the early 1930s the lizard motif was often referred to by her friends as "Dottie's lizards." Although they teased her for "always making lizards" (no. 36, no. 158), some of them later adopted this design for their own baskets. Dottie also pictured the dog and owl on baskets (no. 12, no. 65). She emphasized the owl's

158. *1932*

large eyes by the unusual means of overcast horizontal stitches above and below normal vertical design stitches, thus outlining the eyes. Her butterflies have excellent symmetry and simplicity of form (no. 73, no. 81).

Dottie's life form designs are balanced by geometric motifs, used sparingly in most baskets in a radiating arrangement. Only one basket has an overall geometric pattern (no. 15).

The negative design created by Dottie in basket no. 73, a reversal from the ordinary dark-on-light patterning, is outstanding in its conception. In it the black devil's claw forms the background and light colored willow the design. Negative designs occur occasionally in Supai baskets as isolated elements; including this maker's no. 158, but a basket executed entirely in such a fashion is exceedingly rare.

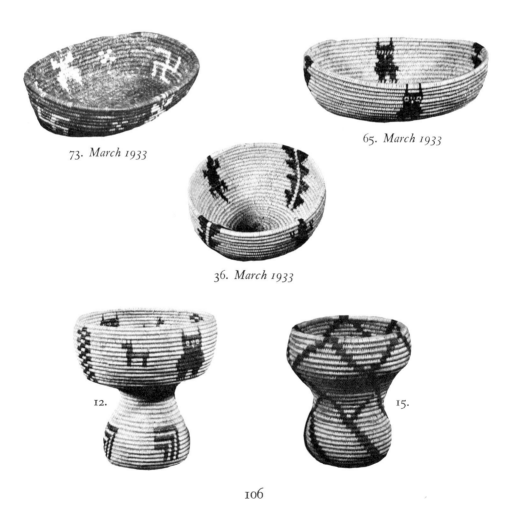

73. *March 1933*

65. *March 1933*

36. *March 1933*

12.

15.

SARAH JONES NODMAN (COOK)
1908–

Sarah's early life was spent mostly in Supai, with some time at Grand Canyon village in the 1930s. Later, she married Bert Cook, a Hualapai, and they moved to Peach Springs, Arizona. Sarah has eight children and several grandchildren.

Because her mother, Gentle Annie, died early, Sarah learned basketmaking by watching other weavers. Her output, never great, included bowls and some small ollas during the 1930s. She gave up basketmaking for a time, but started again in 1971. Now she makes a few plaques when she is able to gather materials—devil's claw from Supai and cottonwood from many locations. She has never made twined baskets, and laughs as she explains that she "never can make the sticks come out even."

THE CIRCULAR BOWLS made by Sarah Nodman in 1933 and 1934 have nicely curved, open-mouthed and globular shapes. Bowl no. 60 is larger than normal and has extra fine stitching (twenty-four per inch). Four blocks of design extend up the walls of each basket. The repeated motifs of no. 47 are described by the maker as "like a diamond." On no. 76 the paired, zigzag elements "look like lightning." Sarah's swastika is "a real Supai design," which she noticed on rocks in Havasu Canyon (probably petroglyphs).

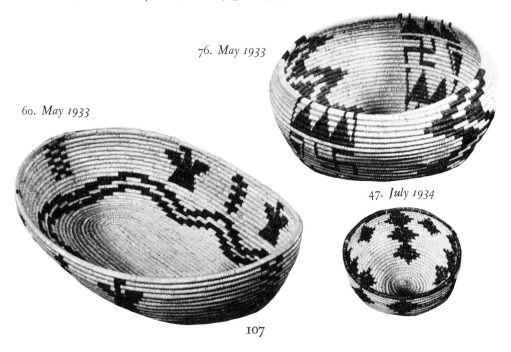

76. *May 1933*

60. *May 1933*

47. *July 1934*

107

IRENE SINYELLA WALEMA
1905–1973

Irene Sinyella Walema was born "under a cottonwood tree" in Supai in 1905. She attended Haskell Institute in Lawrence, Kansas, for four years. She did not begin basketmaking until after her marriage to a Hualapai man, when she was taught by her maternal great-grandmother.

In her later years Irene made no coiled baskets but often made small twined types and both miniature and full-sized cradleboards. In 1973 she remarked that it was hard to get the mesquite roots necessary for her cradles. Willow was more easily obtained, and she especially like to gather it at Supai in October when the twigs are easily bent.

FIGURE 40. Irene Walema with children at McKee home in Grand Canyon, 1934.

CONCERNING THE DESIGNS on her coiled baskets, Irene Walema said they were either "made up out of [her] head" or copied from old baskets. Her sole piece in this collection, tray no. 98, probably does not represent her best coiled work. The pattern is notably off-balance, but the basket has several interesting features, such as the double negative meander motif (a variation of that in Dottie Watahomigie's no. 158), the unusual broadly-ticked rim, and the grey, rather than black, color of the devil's claw used in the design.

98.

ELLA COONEY KASKA
birth date unknown—died about 1942

Ella Kaska was a Hualapai married to Arthur Kaska, a Supai. Ella made good coiled baskets in the manner of the Supais when she lived among them in the 1930s.

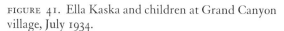
FIGURE 41. Ella Kaska and children at Grand Canyon village, July 1934.

THE WORKMANSHIP on Ella Kaska's baskets was referred to by another basketmaker in the following comment: "I think she is all right." Such a conclusion seems justified on the basis of her beautiful plaque, no. 172. Though not exceedingly fine-textured, the weave is even and close. Two wide bands of outlined, stepped zigzags form a striking composition, well suited to the basket's size. The five points of the inner zigzag form a star-like figure, but six points occur on all of the outer layers. This asymmetry, however, is hardly noticeable in the finished pattern.

Ella is said sometimes to have used in her baskets sewing elements that had been dyed, following the Hualapai style. This feature is not shown in her basket in this collection, however.

172. *July 1934*

PAULINE WEPO WATAHOMIGIE
birth date unknown—died about 1940

Pauline Watahomigie was a Hualapai who lived at the Supai village as a young girl. She married a Supai, Elmer Watahomigie, and moved with him to the south rim of the Grand Canyon when he began work for the National Park Service.

During most of the 1930s Elmer and Pauline lived at the Supai camp near Grand Canyon village. The houses at the camp in those days were very primitive and uncomfortable. When questioned as to what time she had gotten out of bed one cold winter morning, Pauline replied, "At five o'clock." "But why?" "Tired of staying in bed." "What did you do in the cold and the dark?" "Just sat."

Pauline died sometime around 1940. Many years after that Elmer was lost in a storm in the canyon and was never found.

Pauline probably learned to make baskets by observing Supai women at work when she was a girl. The baskets she wove while living at the Grand Canyon, many of which were sold to the McKees, are of excellent quality.

FIGURE 42. Pauline Watahomigie with Ella Kaska (left) and children at McKee home, Grand Canyon, October 1934.

TECHNICALLY, Pauline Watahomigie's baskets are typical of Havasupai workmanship. However, the boldness of the patterns, an effect created by the sparse use of heavy motifs on an uncluttered background, and the unusual nature of the designs make her work distinctive.

Pauline is the only basketmaker known to have used the mountain sheep design. This motif, beautifully executed, appears on basket no. 74. She was also one of the few basketmakers utilizing the duck (no. 64) and the butterfly (ends of no. 74) motifs. Also, some of her geometric motifs are uncommon, as, for example, the cog-like center of no. 154 and the outlined, linearly-arranged triangles of no. 39. The unusual central figures of no. 125 have not yet been identified.

Basket no. 39 has strange features which indicate that it is unfinished. It probably was meant to be a much larger bowl or, more likely, a jar. The shape is oddly attenuated, the small "L"s at the rim appear like feet of uncompleted human figures, and the rim reaches an end with blunt abruptness.

125. *February 1936*

135. *June 1934*

39. *May 1932*

64. *1932*

74. *January 1933*

154. *May 1935*

MAMIE KASKA WATAHOMIGIE (CHIKAPANYGA)
1905–

Mamie Watahomigie was the wife of Joseph Watahomigie in the 1930s, but is now known as Mamie Chick since her marriage to Chikapanyga.

In the 1930s Mamie made her home in Supai. Her father was half-Hualapai. Her mother, Tevaya Jones Jack, was Supai and an excellent basketmaker. It was from her that Mamie learned the rudiments of basket weaving. Mamie herself became well known among the Supais for the excellence of her baskets. She made many in the '30s and won a prize for one of them.

On one occasion Mamie visited the McKee home and saw a large jar-shaped Yavapai basket which stood twenty-six inches high. She was greatly interested in this basket and wanted to know how much it cost. When she learned the amount that had been paid for it—a not inconsiderable sum in those days—she decided to make a similar basket. The one she produced (no. 6) was so well made that she commanded a similar price even though it was much smaller than the Yavapai basket.

In recent years Mamie has made her home in Peach Springs, Arizona. She occasionally visits relatives in Supai, going by helicopter as she no longer is able to ride a horse down the trail.

FIGURE 43. Mamie Watahomigie visits McKee home at Grand Canyon, April 1934.

"SHE MADE GOOD BASKETS," a Supai recently said of Mamie—a real understatement, for her work is outstanding. The jar form, difficult to execute, is perfectly developed in baskets no. 1 and no. 6, and the same mastery of curving surfaces is expressed in the wide-mouthed oval bowls. The trays are essentially flat or slightly curving near the rims. More of her baskets are large rather than small and the oval tray is exceptionally large.

A high quality of work is characteristic of Mamie's basketry. Close, regular stitches number seventeen to nineteen per inch. The even coils are six or seven to the inch, except in the largest baskets which have heavier coiling. The finest texture of twenty stitches per inch occurs in bowl no. 59.

Among the most spectacular designs in the collection are those on jar no. 6

67. *May 1935*

69. *April 1935*

102.

59. *March 1934*

116

and tray no. 147, pieces that are so well matched that they might form a set. Lines of "arrowheads" and double frets enclose extremely well-executed animal and human figures. Front views show both men and women, with arms up or down. Horses with long tails and deer with short tails are arranged on the tray with the greatest attention to symmetry, even to the opposite facing of the animals. The basketmaker said that these designs had no particular meaning. "I made these things so it would look pretty."

Mamie Watahomigie is much given to designs with bold encircling bands and centered flowers (no. 133) or stars (no. 102). Almost all of her linear motifs are paired, whether encircling or placed vertically. The unfinished swastikas on no. 173 are unusual.

In addition to coiled ware, Mamie Watahomigie made cradleboards and twined ware, two beautiful examples of which are shown in no. 163 and no. 165 in the section on *Utilitarian Ware*.

147. *April 1934*

1.

133. *July 1939*

6. *June 1933*

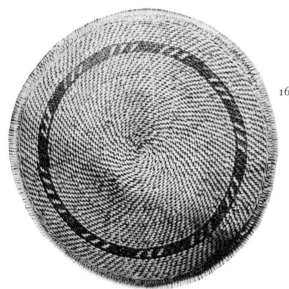

163. *Utility Basket, diameter 14″*

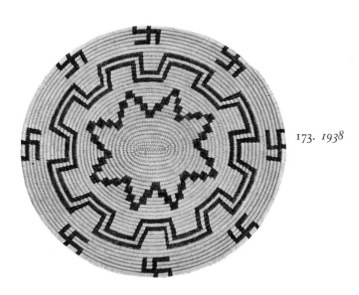

173. *1938*

LILY WODO BURRO
1893–1969

Lilly Burro attended the school in Havasu Canyon for only a few years. Later she was employed for some time as a cook at the school and also often aided the schoolmistress with the children, but she never learned to speak fluent English.

In the early 1930s Lilly lived at Grand Canyon village. During this time she became the first Supai woman to help with the housework in the McKee home there. She was very willing and always cheerful.

After her residence on the south rim of Grand Canyon she and her husband, Billy Burro, moved back to the Supai village. They lived there and at times at Pasture Wash, near the head of the Topocoba trail, for many years. Billy Burro was a policeman in Supai; he also was one of the early mail carriers. In those days only first class mail was delivered and it was trucked over a difficult, primitive road to the head of the Topocoba trail, then packed on horses to Supai post office. After Billy's death in 1950, Lilly lived in a primitive hut near Minnie Marshall's house. Minnie gave her food and guided her around the premises when Lilly's eyesight failed. Later Lilly stayed with Lee and Florence Marshall, who cared for her until her death in 1969.

As a basketmaker, Lilly Burro restricted her activities to making the twined type of basket. She produced a few of these at the time she was living at Grand Canyon village in the early 1930s and probably continued later. Unfortunately none of her baskets are in the collection.

FIGURE 44. Lilly Burro on South Rim, Grand Canyon, 1930.

FIGURE 45. Lilly Burro at her home in Havasu Canyon, 1941.

TECQUEMIJA KASKA MONTOYA
1870– date of death unknown

Tecquemija Montoya, more often called by her nickname Susie, was the wife of Supai Shorty. This elderly couple made their home on the south rim of Grand Canyon in the early 1930s when Shorty was working as a laborer for the National Park Service. Susie made both coiled and twined baskets and water containers of large size which she sold to the Grand Canyon curio stores and to local residents.

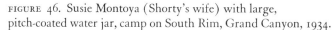

FIGURE 46. Susie Montoya (Shorty's wife) with large, pitch-coated water jar, camp on South Rim, Grand Canyon, 1934.

THE JARS PRODUCED by Susie Montoya are large enough (approximately twenty to twenty-four inches high) to have held at least five gallons of water. They are flat-bottomed and deeply cylindrical, with wide mouths to facilitate dipping from them. Because they were completely waterproofed with aromatic pinyon pitch, they made admirable reservoirs in which to keep the domestic water of a household.

FIGURE 47. Supai Shorty Montoya with pitch-covered jar, Grand Canyon, October 1934.

YEWAIA [Heart] CHEYUT PAKETEKOPA
1860– date of death unknown

Yewaia and her husband, Wilman Paketekopa, arrived at the McKee residence one summer morning in 1935 with a large collection of water jars of all sizes. Yewaia did not speak any English, so her husband acted as her interpreter. So far as is known, Yewaia made only twined baskets.

168. 1935 Diameter 6⅞"
Height 11¾"

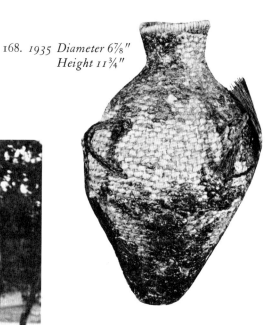

FIGURE 48. Yewaia Paketekopa visits Grand Canyon village with pitch-coated water bottles on back and wearing old type shoes, November 1935.

124

THE WATER JARS of this elderly weaver show the wide range of form and size still being produced and used by some Havasupais in 1935. The largest, about twenty inches high, has the flat bottom and wide mouth best suited to a storage vessel. Others are much smaller, canteen-like containers with globular or biconical bodies, short, narrow necks and small mouths (no. 168). They are provided with braided horsehair loops, to which carrying straps can be fastened for carrying on one's back as shown in the photograph, or from a saddle. The photograph illustrates how this biconical form provides not only a comfortable fit on the back in carrying position, but also a non-spill resting position for the jar.

FIGURE 49. Yewaia and Wilman Paketekopa with assorted water bottles made by Yewaia, November 1935.

TASCHIGVA HAMIDREEK* BIG JIM
1870–1946

"Old Lady Susie" is said to have made baskets the old way, including the use of dye and the forming of "all kinds of shapes." An informant recently explained that she also commonly tied on buckskin to make a narrow handle fastened to the rim coil.

Two baskets in the collection, attributed to Old Lady Susie by Viola Crook, Ethel Jack, and Minnie Marshall, are deep forms of distinctive character. No other Supai basketmaker, to our knowledge, has the deep truncated-cone shape of no. 7. Ten paired "trails" emphasize the great depth of this, the largest bowl in the collection. Bowl no. 184, although small, is exceptionally deep for its size.

*At the time Taschigva bore the name "Hamidreek" it was pronounced *Hamtecq* [Nighthawk]. Note from Steve Hirst, tribal recorder.

184.

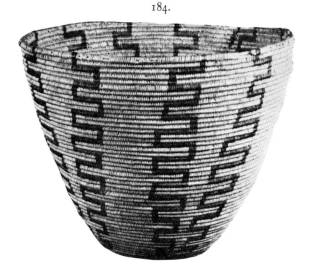

7.

UTILITARIAN WARE
Water Jars, Parching Trays, Burden Baskets, Cradle Boards

WATER JARS. Water jars, covered with the pitch of pinyon pine, were still extensively made and used by the Havasupai in the 1930's. They were of many different sizes and shapes, ranging up to twenty-four inches or more in height, and ten inches in diameter. Some of the larger ones were used as water storage vessels, whereas others, with narrow necks and small mouths, served as canteens or water carriers and were provided with braided horsehair loops and carrying straps. In order not to lose any more than necessary of the precious water in them, in case of a spill, many of the canteens were made with conical bases.

By virtue of having lost most of its original pitched exterior, a jar made by Mamie Watahomigie (no. 165) shows clearly the twined construction of a typical water jar. Diagonal twining forms the basis of the wall, but rows of three-strand twining, with its longer and stronger stitches, reinforce the base, midsection and neck. In a completed jar the resulting attractive variation of texture becomes obscured by the red or brown pitch.

Jar no. 164 has a bucket shape, with the mouth as wide as the waist (nine inches). Its unknown maker provided two very effective, braided horsehair handles, running horizontally for two and three-quarters inches on opposite sides near the rim. Another uncommon shape is the hourglass, or double jar (no. 169), more than fifteen inches high.

165. Mamie Watahomigie
April 1934
Diameter 7"
Height 10½"

169.
Diameter 6¾"
Height 15½"

164.
Diameter 9"
Height 12½"

166. *Susie Jack, March 1936*
Diameter 9⅞"
Height 10½"

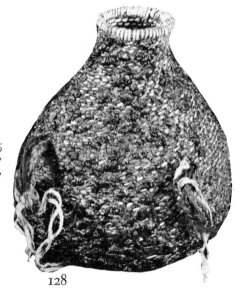

167.
Diameter 6⅞"
Height 9"

168. *Yewiya Paketekopa*
Diameter 6⅞"
Height 11¾"

BURDEN BASKETS. The twined burden basket, or *cathok,* once indispensible in daily life for the collection, transportation, and storage of food materials, continued to be made in small numbers into recent times even though commercial interest in such utility types was small. The older basketmakers in the 1930s, such as Katie Hamidreek, Lina Iditicava, and many others, made fine burden baskets.

Alice Jones produced an excellent example of a burden basket (no. 161). From a pointed base, uniformly straight walls rise 18½ inches to a wide circular mouth almost 22 inches in diameter, forming a conical shape with great strength and capacity. The basket could be carried by a long rawhide strap looped through two five-strand buckskin support loops sewn through the back basket wall, twelve inches apart and at a point two-thirds up the basket.

A cowhide patch, shrunken in place to fit and attached at the edge with running stitches of sinew, insures durability for the burden basket base. Two rows of three-strand twining add strength at the top with a coiling stitch one above the other to form the ring rim.

163. *Mamie Watahomigie*
Diameter 14"

129

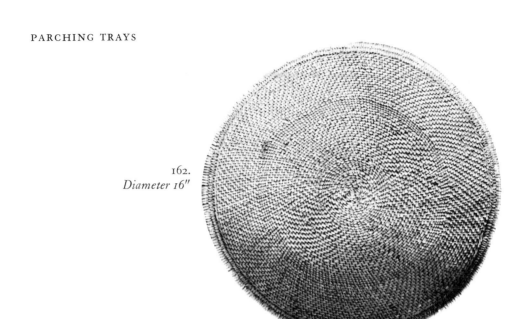

162.
Diameter 16"

174. *Alice Jones, 1938*
Diameter 17½"

Diagonal twining of narrow strips of willow (eight rows per inch) form a beautiful obliquely-textured surface across the basket wall. Encircling design bands are twined in devil's claw at the level of the loops and near the rim. Though very simple, the line of triangles and the narrow fretline make a more prominent pattern than many on such utilitarian baskets.

UTILITY TRAYS AND PARCHING TRAYS. Present day Supai basketmakers say this type of twined basket is "real Indian design." The parching trays made during the 1930s did remain true to the utilitarian design of a lightweight, sturdy, and broad shallow vessel in which seeds might be shaken for winnowing or parching. Those trays made for sale such as no. 162, no. 163, and no. 174, depart from normal only in being more attractive in their unused condition. Many worn serving trays have had a heat-resisting coat of stewed peaches smeared on the inner surface.

Larger than most coiled trays, these trays measure from fourteen to seven-

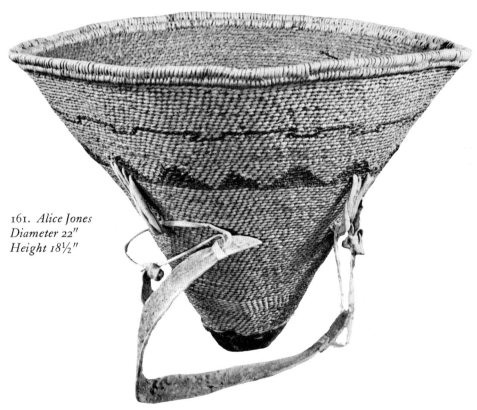

161. *Alice Jones*
Diameter 22″
Height 18½″

teen inches in diameter and about three inches in depth. In no. 162 (unidentified maker) the unadorned form gains a certain beauty through the regular texture of diagonal twining, varied near the center and midway by several bands of plain twining. In those trays by Mamie Watahomigie (no. 163) and Alice Jones (no. 174), the black devil's claw forms the customary banded patterns of diagonally-ticked lines in various arrangements. Other weavers known for their parching trays were Lina Iditicava, Mabel Barney and Katie Hamidreek.

CRADLEBOARDS. Edith Putesoy's baby (fig. 37) is being carried in 1937 in the same way described earlier in the century by Spier (1928, p. 302): "A woman does not carry the cradle much on her back, but more frequently in her arms."

The cradleboard Edith made for the McKees (no. 170) is twenty-six inches long and entirely typical of Supai construction: a bed of sticks is bound across an oval frame, and a curved wicker hood is tied to the upper end. Katie Hamidreek's miniature (no. 171), which is ten inches long, also shows the two tying bands threaded through the four cloth loops. Each woman apparently treated decorative details differently, as illustrated by the ribbon strip ornament added to the wicker hood by Edith.

Cradleboards of the old type are still commonly used today.

FIGURE 50. Irene Walema's baby in cradleboard, 1934.

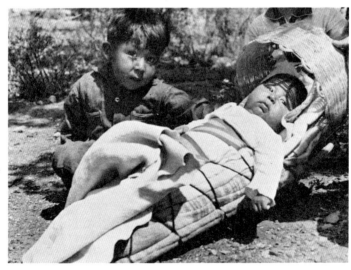

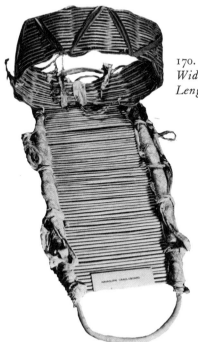

170. *Edith Putesoy*
Width 14″
Length 26″

171. *Katie Hamidreek*
Width 4½″
Length 10″

UNIDENTIFIED COILED BASKETS

During the decade of 1930–1940, while making the collection of Havasupai baskets illustrated in this book, a practice of recording the name of the maker and the date of basket acquisition was followed. This information was recorded with tape on the back of each basket, but unfortunately during subsequent years in which the collection was involved in several house moves and parts of it were transported to two World's Fairs (San Francisco and New York) for exhibit, some of the labels fell off and were lost. Nevertheless, because the un-labelled baskets are a significant part of the collection, represent the work of a known period, and include some exceptionally fine examples of workmanship, they have been included in the book.

35.   72.   30.   75.

A DEEP CIRCULAR BOWL, no. 75 is outstandingly massive. Its fifteen inch maximum diameter makes it one of the largest bowls in the collection and its 3½ coils and 8 stitches per inch represent an extreme in coarseness of texture. Surprisingly, the base has much finer texture. Extra heavy construction also characterizes the broad, low bowl (no. 9).

Exceptionally small are baskets no. 72 (5½ inches long), no. 49 and no. 50 (each 3¼ inches maximum diameter). Basket no. 50 has a curious conical shape and seems to be a miniature burden basket, coiled rather than twined. Baskets no. 41, no. 72 and no. 134 have fine stitching, twenty per inch, and trays no. 79 and no. 149 have coarser texture than average.

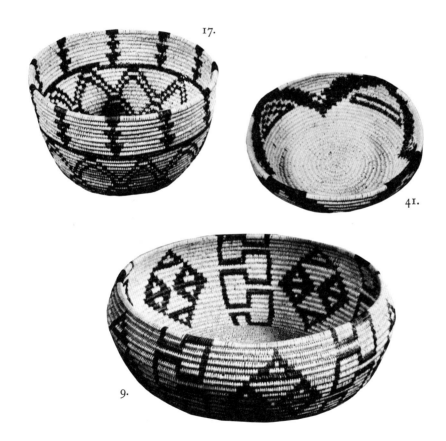

17.

41.

9.

The designs of many different women are represented in these baskets, showing patterns of style as well as individual variations. A clear preference for vertical layout of block and/or linear motifs is shown on bowl walls. Commonly the motifs are paired on opposite sides (e.g. no. 30, no. 50) but in some baskets they are repeated (e.g. no. 17, no. 35). Encircling layouts are few (e.g. no. 17, no. 75). Different basketmakers may change the details of a motif, yet use it very similarly, as is seen in the portrayals of the eagle on no. 30 and no. 72.

Unusual design features in this group of baskets include the outer motifs of no. 134, which were said to resemble "a horse brand," the complex diamond motifs on no. 9, and the "cross-stitch" rim treatment on no. 49. Exceptionally fine patterning of the wings lends distinction to the butterflies on no. 140.

The maker of the large oval tray no. 149 used notably little black in its design and, perhaps in compensation, added an unusual touch of color in a red stepped line following the central black band. Now so much faded that it hardly appears in the photograph, the red originally was a deep hue produced from commercial dye. Lack of black as well as use of dyed color characterize

24.

79.

much Hualapai basketry, and several Supais attribute this example to one of the Hualapai women living among them, saying, "They used dye sometimes."

SOME BASKETMAKERS of the 1930s whose work is not known to be represented in the collection are listed below. Their names have been repeatedly mentioned in interviews.

Molly (Tethecqecha) Mulgulo   (Mecca Uqualla's mother)
Susie (Suteluija) Spoonhead   (Minnie Marshall's grandmother)
Elva Watahomigie*   (Eunice Jones' mother)
Josie Watahomigie   (Edith Putesoy's sister)

*Basketweaver referred to in: McKee, E. D., 1933, Havasupai Basketry: Grand Canyon Nature Notes, vol. 8, no. 1, p. 133.

25.

66.

140.

180.

181.

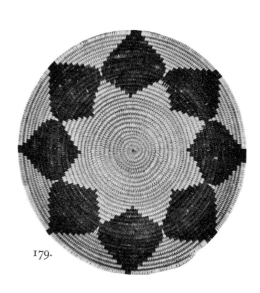

179.

50. *Miniature or toy burden basket*

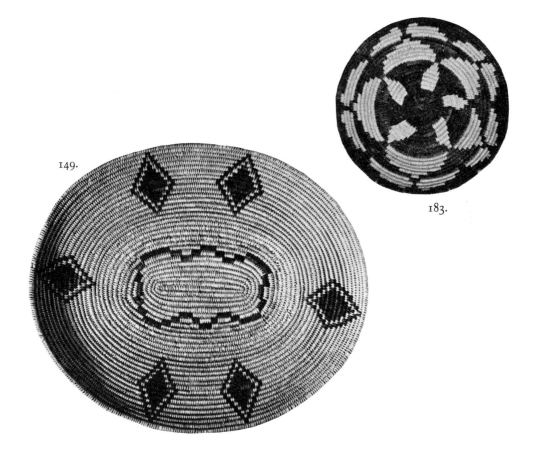

149.

183.

178.

134.

SELECTED REFERENCES ON THE HAVASUPAI

Bateman, Paul, 1972, *Culture change and revival in Pai basketry:* Northern
   Arizona Univ., M.A. thesis.

Casanova, F. E., 1967, Trails to Supai in Cataract Canyon: Plateau, vol. 39, no. 3,
   p. 124–130.

Cushing, F. H., 1887, A study of Pueblo pottery as illustrative of Zuni culture
   growth: Smithsonian Inst., Bur. Am. Ethnology Rept. 4; p. 467–521.

Cushing, F. H., 1965, The Nation of the Willows: Flagstaff, Ariz., Northland
   Press (Reprinted), [from The Atlantic Monthly, 1882, v. 50, p. 362–374, 541–
   559].

Dobyns, H. F., and Euler, R. C., 1971, The Havasupai people: Phoenix, Ariz.,
   Indian Tribal Ser., Flagstaff, Ariz., Northland Press, 71 p.

Douglas, F. H., 1931, The Havasupai Indians: Denver Art Mus. Leaflet 33, 4 p.

Euler, R. C., 1970, Prehistoric man in the Grand Canyon, *in* Goldwater, B. M.,
   Delightful journey down the Green and Colorado rivers: Tempe, Ariz.,
   Arizona Hist. Found., p. 102–105.

Griffin, J. I., 1972, Today with the Havasupai Indians: Indian Tribal Ser.,
   [Flagstaff, Ariz., Northland Press], Phoenix, Ariz., 32 p.

Hughes, J. D., 1967, The story of man at Grand Canyon: Grand Canyon Nat.
   History Assoc. Bull. 14, 195 p.

Iliff, F. G., 1954, People of the Blue Water; My adventures among the Walapai
   and Havasupai Indians: New York, Harper and Bros.,

James, G. W., 1903, Indian basketry and how to make Indian and other baskets:
   Printed by the author, Pasadena, Calif.

Kelly, W. H., 1953, Indians of the Southwest: 1st Ann. Rept., Bur. Ethnic Research, Tucson, Ariz.

McKee, E. D., 1933, Havasupai basketry: Grand Canyon Nature Notes, v. 8, no.
   1, p. 130–135.

Mason, O. T., 1904, Aboriginal American basketry: Studies in a textile art without machinery: Smithsonian Inst., Ann. Rept. for year ending June 30, 1902,
   p. 171–548.

Robinson, Bert, 1954, The basket weavers of Arizona: New Mexico Univ. Press,
   164 p.

Schwartz, D. W., 1956, The Havasupai 600 A.D.–1955 A.D.—A short culture history: Plat., v. 28, no. 4, p. 77–85.

————, 1957, Climate change and culture history in the Grand Canyon region; Am. Antiquity, v. 22, no. 4, pt. 1, p. 372–377.

————, 1959, Culture area and time depth—The Four Worlds of the Havasupai: Am. Anthropologist, v. 61, p. 1060–1070.

Smithson, C. L., 1959, The Havasupai Woman: Utah Univ. Anthropol. Papers, no. 38, 170 p.

Spier, Leslie, 1928, Havasupai ethnography: Am. Mus. Nat. History, Anthropol. Papers v. 29, pt. 3, 392 p.

Tanner, C. L., 1968, Southwest Indian craft arts: Tucson, Ariz., Arizona Univ. Press.

Wampler, Joseph, 1959, Havasu Canyon—Gem of the Grand Canyon: Berkeley, Calif., Howell-North, 121 p.

Whiting, A. F., 1942, Havasupai habitat: Unpub. manuscript on file and available for inspection in the Mus. Northern Arizona.